ONE DAY
I WILL UNDERSTAND

JANE TURPIN

This is a photo of our beautiful daughter

Naomi

Foreword

I feel privileged to have been asked to write a foreword for my friend Jane's book 'One day I will understand.' I have known Jane for many years and heartily recommend you read her family's story to date! I know that she has worked hard at putting pen to paper in available moments, while caring, with her husband, for their daughter Naomi, who is now a young adult with learning difficulties.

In this book, Jane has written of her own family's experiences and of a small gravestone in their village churchyard. She has gradually learned to trust God on a day-to-day basis, whatever happens. This is something to which we can all relate, as we face our own differing, difficult situations. We all have our own "Why" questions, for which we await the answers.

Jane's personal faith in the Lord Jesus Christ, through His death for our sin, and resurrection, eventually shines through. She finishes her book with her own conclusions as to how we too can find Him, repent of our sin, and trust Him for ourselves.

Faith Gage

Acknowledgments

'One day I will understand'

I would like to thank everyone who has helped me in the writing of this book — all the people who have patiently read, and re–read, my manuscript. I am so grateful for their tremendous support and kindness in helping to make this book a reality. I especially thank Faith and Teresa, for their suggestions.

I am so grateful for my friends Frances, Paula and Cindy, who have always been there for me. I would also like to thank Helen for her assistance with the publishing of this book and Ruth Richards for her painting of the roses. It is greatly appreciated. Unless specified otherwise, all Bible quotations are from the New International Version (prior to its 2011 revision).

Apart from the Lord, most of all I thank my husband Paul for his patience and forbearance whilst I have been writing this story. I cannot thank you enough, Paul, for looking after Naomi and therefore letting me finish the book. Time after time, I have delayed putting into practice what I believe the Lord has called me to do. I am so thankful I serve a faithful God, who knows our hearts. With His help, we need never give up and therefore can be assured of eventually achieving our goals.

I would like to say that, due to sensitive information, I have changed some people's names and have given fictional names to certain places.

This book is about my life, the highs and the lows of it. Why do bad things happen in life and what is God trying to say to us in it all? I don't profess to have all the answers, but one thing I do know since coming to know the Lord -- He is good and one day I will understand, hence the title of my book.

Contents

Introduction

I looked up. I took the dark haired child into my arms. She seemed so perfect, so pretty. I could hardly believe it. We called her Naomi. God had granted us my heart's desire and finally given my husband and me a child to treasure. It was almost too good to be true.

Was this child really ours to keep and nurture? It seemed like a miracle. Indeed, as far as I was concerned, it *was* a miracle!

Chapter One

My early life

I was born on the 4th of July in 1953 in Brentwood, Essex. After my birth, I returned with my parents to live a few miles away in the small town of Billericay. My memories of this time are very sketchy and somewhat blurred as I was very young.

My father had been a pacifist during the war. He met my mother when working as a casual farm labourer for her father. Born in London, from a working class background, his parents were reasonably 'well off' compared to some others in a similar position. His parents had run a fish and chip shop for many years and undoubtedly had worked hard for a living. His grandfather had been a policeman, until invalided out of the force after being injured when intervening in a burglary. Fortunately, the property he had tried to defend, in spite of being off duty, belonged to a wealthy gentleman who saw fit to compensate my great-grandfather and his family. I would hasten to point out that none of this is proven fact and so I cannot be sure of the truth, but it may account for my grandfather's relative inherited wealth. Later my great-grandfather ran a pub in Ongar.

My father managed to acquire a small nursery, which mainly focused on producing tomatoes. In late 1957, my father was offered a job in a very rural part of East Anglia as a tenant farmer, which he accepted.

My brother, Paul, and I were fortunate to be brought up on a farm. Paul was about three years my senior and together we took turns feeding the baby lambs and enjoyed visiting the piglets and the cows. This idyll changed, however, when my brother went away to boarding school, leaving me on the farm. I grew up very much like an only child and can fully empathise with such individuals.

Life for my mother had not been easy either since our move away from Billericay. She felt isolated and distant from the life she had known -- separated from family and friends in this completely new life. At first she had wondered if she'd be able to adjust to such a significant change in her circumstances but, given time, she grew to love the area, and was quite content.

At five years old, I started education at the local primary school. After about two years it was decided I wasn't making the expected progress as, unfortunately, I had had to miss out on a lot of school due to a range of unforeseen circumstances.

When I was about six, I had been teasing the collie farm dog when it turned on me. Moss, the dog, savaged me -- biting off most of my right eyebrow. I still remember the blood gushing out of the new wound as if it were yesterday. The whole incident, on that February afternoon, is not far from my mind even now. After visiting our local hospital about twenty miles away, I was transferred to the well-known Mount Vernon hospital in Middlesex. It was 1960; parents were only allowed to visit their children twice a week, on a Sunday and Wednesday. I felt lost and alone. Visit days became the highlight of my young life and were all I could focus on at this dark time. I remained at Mount Vernon for about a month, a long time and a long way away from my family -- hard for any child to experience. When I was discharged from Mount Vernon, I needed to be constantly reviewed in the outpatients department at my local hospital. With the skill of the surgeons, I healed well physically and the scar is not very noticeable after all these years. Moss went on to maul two other children and, as a result, had to be put down.

A few months after the Moss incident was over, I had to go to the local hospital for an operation on a squint. I previously had to attend the outpatient eye clinic and have eye drops in my eyes, something I totally dreaded. I was also advised to wear an eye patch over my good eye, which I found equally unwelcome. I cannot remember if other children teased me, but I was certainly self-conscious of it. Fortunately for me, my local hospital was more relaxed about allowing children to receive visitors than Mount Vernon had been.

To this day, a beautiful memory stands out amongst these awful experiences. My Dad picked me up from the hospital and, just before going home, we walked to a nearby toyshop. In there I selected a delightful doll that I later named Catherine. As I recall this memory so many years later, it still brings a lump to my throat. I realise just how very special it was to me, what it still means to the little 'child' in me.

I had also suffered a term off school with whooping cough around this period in my life, which naturally did not help a child who was already struggling at school.

As a result of my slow progress, my Auntie Sheila suggested that I might benefit from attending another school and my parents agreed. I did not fully understand the implications of what this meant and didn't see the suggestion as any kind of threat. It meant travelling about thirteen miles away to a convent school. Initially, parents would take it in turns to take different children to their respective schools, but eventually this came to an end and we made the journey by bus instead.

Soon after I began at the convent school, I realised I was in a class one year younger than my proper age, but this did not make me feel inadequate. I was having problems, but I failed to see the situation in the way that adults perceived it.

Happily I made friends but, despite this, I was beginning to feel 'different.' I especially found it hard to play simple ball games and wondered why I couldn't adapt and 'fit in' like the other children. One day, I was in school and my knickers fell down. I could have died. Why did these things happen to me? Why was I the odd one out? I certainly didn't see the funny side of it.

My mother, God bless her, did her best to teach me. She patiently taught me to read the Janet and John books and practise my handwriting. Nevertheless, she was disappointed that I was what the education system at that time considered to be 'backward' and not making the grade. One of my teachers, not a nun, thought I was a spastic, but my father strongly refuted this.

Still, despite all my difficulties in learning, I was put forward for the Eleven Plus exam. I was not happy about this, but whether or not I expressed this verbally to the adults I cannot recall. I felt that I was not suitable for such an exam and fear of failure was uppermost in my mind. Paul had passed the first part of the Eleven Plus, but had failed the second part (a common occurrence back then). However, I did not even feel ready for the first part. What I feared became a reality: I failed the exam. My confidence, if it ever had been there, ebbed away. This was my first true encounter with failure.

I was also aware that I was in a Catholic environment and there were occasions when the nuns' presence made me afraid. Still, overall, I was treated kindly and fairly. I did find their religious activities daunting and felt somewhat detached from whatever they were trying to convey. I was thankful, as a Protestant, that I was not expected to learn the Catechism. I did become accustomed to singing in Latin, however, and learned a lot about the dead saints, Saint Francis of Assisi being my favourite. Yet the Bible, to the best of my knowledge, was never mentioned, apart from the hymn '*The King of love, my shepherd is*,' where I could see *Psalm 23* hidden in the background.

I loved the school holidays as they meant having my big brother home with me. I welcomed climbing trees in the orchard, playing in the haystack, and going to the next-door farm, by then abandoned as the house and cottages had fallen into disrepair. It was a haven for youngsters to explore. I liked the excitement of it, imagining our neighbours shooting us for trespassing if we were found at 'Old Den'. As well as the farm, there was an island positioned in a pond, which thrilled me with its very existence. It was a break from the mundane. There were so many different places just waiting to be discovered by us children and playing 'hide and seek' was another popular activity.

One of the highlights in my young life was the annual holiday we took in August. We usually spent the first night with my Auntie Sheila and her husband Uncle Gerald in London. My father stayed at home to look after the farm. However my mother, Auntie Sheila, Paul and my two cousins, Diane and Stuart, rose at five o'clock in the morning to travel down to Swanage in Dorset. There were no motorways then, but we would arrive at Swanage about twelve noon. On the way, we would travel through the New Forest to see the famous ponies. I enjoyed playing on the beach, swimming in the sea, visiting the caves and going to Corfe Castle.

One year my Dad, who had recently learnt to ski, took Paul and Diane to Aviemore in Scotland for a skiing holiday, which they loved. When I was about eleven I was introduced to holidays abroad and we went, in both the summer and winter, to a beautiful area in Switzerland situated high up in the mountains in a village known as Champery. I commenced skiing myself and, although I haven't skied for many years, it is like riding a bicycle. You never forget.

One day when I was about seven, just before Christmas, I was horrified to find our old barn and the pig sheds on fire. The barn had been a place of retreat and escape for my dolls and me. We loved our personal space in the loft of the old barn. It was where we could get away from everyday life. Suddenly, something I had deeply treasured had gone. I was more upset for myself than the pigs, I have to admit. The fire was probably caused by an electric lamp falling down and catching alight in the pigs' shed, with the flames in turn spreading to the barn. Eventually a new barn was built on the site, but it did not compensate for what I had lost. I discovered later in my young life, however, that the new barn was great for roller-skating and the freedom and excitement we experienced, even now, captivates my memories.

I had another unexpected, unwelcome incident about a year before I left primary school. My father was a member of the Freemasons and, every year in May, an annual event was held at Ramsgate in Kent. My grandparents attended, as did my Auntie Sheila and Uncle Gerald with their children Diane and Stuart. We would be served a large eight-course, leisurely meal that I always enjoyed, followed by dancing. The dancing did not finish until midnight, although I could never stay to the end because of my age. One year, when I was nearly ten, I asked my mother and aunt if I could be there until midnight, as I was growing up fast and it seemed a reasonable thing to do. The only obstacle that stood in my way was that my younger cousin Stuart might have felt excluded, thinking he should be allowed to stay up too. I felt uncomfortable about this. The adults assured me I could tell a 'white lie', but I instinctively knew this was not right -- a lie is a lie, whatever we may say to justify it. Still, I went against my conscience just the same and danced till midnight.

The Bible says "*A man reaps what he sows*" (*Galatians 6:7*).

Early next morning I awoke to a strange unfamiliar nightmare. My face was twitching and I was fitting. My grandfather was quickly called, as he had received some medical training in first aid when he had been a soldier in the First World War. I remember him taking my pulse and saying I was fine. No one knew what had happened to me. It was a complete mystery and was put down to tiredness. Yet, I felt I knew the reason why! God was punishing me for lying. I had done wrong and this was the price I had to pay. Now, as an adult and with the benefit of hindsight, such an assumption is probably false. Needless to say though, at that young age, the penalties for lying assumed gigantic proportions. I realised, even as a non-believer that we humans *know* right from wrong, so are without excuse.

It was hoped I would have no further seizures, but I did and the neurologist confirmed I had 'petit mal' a mild form of epilepsy. This, once again, left me with the feeling of being different from other people. I became ridiculously 'sensitive' to the fact that I was now on tablets to control my epilepsy -- so much so that, as we started to holiday abroad, I dreaded the customs officers rummaging throughout our suitcases in case they discovered my epileptic tablets. This seems laughable to me now, but at the time there was nothing anyone could say to ease my embarrassment. I could not overcome these 'paranoid' feelings.

Around this time I had another major upset in my life. I woke up one morning to find that my father, whom I adored, was not at home. What had happened to him? I was informed that he was very ill. I felt instantly lost and betrayed. How could Dad do this to me? Good, old, reliable Dad - it just wasn't possible. I burst into tears, feeling alone and hopeless.

My father was diagnosed with a mystery illness and, to this day, we don't know what it was. The doctors had no idea what was wrong with him and placed him in an isolation hospital. My brother and I were only allowed to see Dad through the window. We never discovered whether he had become ill through working with cows on the farm, or whether an inoculation he had been given had resulted in him becoming seriously ill. Eventually though, given time, Dad made a full recovery and I thank the good Lord for His kindness and compassion for healing my father when He did.

At this point I would like to describe my father's character. He had one sister, Auntie Sheila, making his a relatively small family for those times. He was a very kind, outgoing and caring person. He was also intelligent and loved people. Most people enjoyed his company. He coped well with the demands of life and was gifted with all things practical. As a youngster, my father had excelled at tennis and there had even been talk of him playing at Wimbledon, though this did not come to pass. He played golf and, with my uncle, started skiing at the age of forty-two, which was considered 'old' back in the nineteen sixties. My father's main fault was that, at times, he allowed himself to be 'dictated to' by my mother's dominant personality. Yet he was a gem and someone I loved dearly.

Mum had a strong, determined character and was well known to be 'a real worrier'. Mother came from a well-off, some would say, privileged background. Her father, as already mentioned, was a farmer. Both her parents were originally from Lancashire and had moved to East Anglia in the early twentieth century. Mum was one of five children (two boys and three girls) and, unlike her sisters, had never had to work for a living. In the Second World War, as a young unmarried woman, she had acted as a housekeeper for her parents and for one brother and his family, to meet their various needs. Some folk considered Mother to have lived a sheltered life. She was also considered by most people to be rather naïve and gullible when it came to jokes, however she did well at school and left with eight matriculations for her efforts. She liked people to be intelligent, but in other ways she had a heart of gold.

Although, for me, life was often far from easy, people could say I had an idyllic childhood. When I was about ten, my grandfather invested in his grandchildren by buying a pony for us. Another pony and a horse quickly followed. I should have been grateful, but for me there was a void in my life that I could never seem to fill. Paul did not have a passion for riding either! Of course he was at boarding school, but I doubt if this had much influence regarding the way he felt about horses. Yet Diane and Stuart, who lived in London, were totally different. Diane took to riding like a duck to water. All four of us cousins went to riding school and eventually learnt to ride independently. I remember one particular day with shame -- I cruelly teased a young girl who was learning to ride. She had Down's syndrome and I teased her because of her disability. I can offer no excuses for my callous act. I can only conclude I did this to try to alleviate my own feelings of inferiority and inadequacy.

I still felt I stood out like a sore thumb and I was struggling with my overall confidence. I allowed myself to succumb to fear and seemed incapable of putting the bridle and bit into the pony's mouth. I refused to tackle my fear 'head on' and regret this even now. However, I learned to trot, canter and even gallop and, at times, I enjoyed myself horse riding.

I recall one Field Day event when I was a teenager. This was a well-known farmers' activity in the sixties. This particular year it was held at our farm and included a Gymkhana. I had to participate in a horse jumping competition. I had not been disciplined about practising beforehand, which put me in poor stead for the competition. I found myself being humiliated, as my pony refused to jump the fences. I came last and felt a failure for the umpteenth time. Naturally, Diane did well and came away with a rosette.

The years went by and I was moved to a private mixed school called Clark's College. The school focused mainly on shorthand and typing for girls, with the emphasis on becoming secretaries one day. The idea of becoming a secretary did not appeal to me and I fantasised about doing something altogether more exciting and thrilling.

I had not been long at Clark's College when my eye specialist informed my mother that I needed glasses for short sightedness. I was advised to wear them all the time. I burst into tears, firmly in denial of what was being said. I did not want to know. I dreaded the comments of other children and tried to delude myself that it was not happening to me. As I have already said, I loved my dad, but I had certainly never wanted to inherit his short sightedness. I felt jealous that my brother's eyes were fine and I was the one once again being singled out as 'different.' Some of the girls at school tried to encourage me to wear my glasses in class, but I remained fearful of being teased. I needed to sit near the blackboard, or copy from my classmate's books. I was teased about my glasses, getting the standard 'four eyes' taunts but, with hindsight, I realise *the fear* of being teased was my phobia. The fear was far worse than what happened in reality. In some ways, I wish now I could have my time over again and give each one of my fears to my Lord. I am sure it would have helped, but of course I did not know I could do this then.

We were a 'church going' family, however. We would often go to the local Anglican Church on Sundays. My mother was a staunch believer in God and the Christian faith, to the outsider seeming very committed to the church. In her early years she had sung in the choir and naturally blended into the familiarity and form of service in this setting. Meantime, I struggled to read from the prayer book. God seemed distant and far away. I believed in *something*, but wasn't sure exactly what. We read from the prayer book that "*He has filled the hungry with good things, but has sent the rich away empty*" (*Luke 1:53*). In my innocence I literally interpreted this as meaning that for some reason, known only to our precious Lord, the physically hungry people would now have enough to eat, but the people with money would instead become poor and hungry. This did not seem right and I left feeling confused and somewhat bewildered. Of course I was failing to grasp the spiritual meaning of the verse.

My Mum was proud of the fact she had encouraged Dad to become more involved in the church, partly taking credit for his becoming a churchwarden. As a young child I had been acquainted with some of the stories of the Bible. I especially treasured the stories of Jesus healing children in my familiar child's Bible and, when I visited Diane and Stuart, I was particularly drawn to Stuart's rather large Bible. I knew there was something special about this book, but at the time what it was eluded me.

I especially loved the Christmas stories in God's Word and singing carols. Every year my family and I would join other carol singers and travel around the local village in a trailer pulled by a tractor, singing our hearts out. The atmosphere was magical and electric. I was proud that I knew most of the carols by heart. This time of year filled me with hope, and a joy explicit to this particular season.

At my new school, I was now interacting with children of my own age. I was no longer the eldest in the class, but one of the youngest. Nevertheless, my problems with schoolwork were still very evident and I was constantly either at the bottom of the class or near to the bottom. I felt a failure academically, but there was one occasion I recall with great delight. I managed to come seventh in the class that particular term and it was a moment of great excitement and jubilation. I also received a prize for making the most progress over the year. I could hardly believe my ears! I was now in the privileged position of being able to choose what I would like as a reward. One of the gifts mentioned was a book on Scotland and, as I loved mountains and beautiful scenery, I readily chose this. Even now that sweet memory is close to my heart.

Yet, despite this, I was far from happy at school. I continued to struggle in the classroom. The boys in my class teased me. My surname was Dicker and I was constantly called 'Tick tock'. As I grew older, I was tormented because I was very naïve about sex and the facts of life. My mother, God bless her, had failed to discuss these important issues with me. I guess, to be fair to Mum, that sort of attitude was commonplace in the sixties.

I found intermingling with some girls tense and difficult. There was one who travelled on my train, who I will name Brenda. I suppose one would call our relationship 'a personality clash' today. We were forever arguing and making life unpleasant for each other.

My relationship with my French teacher, too, was far from perfect and the friction that existed between us did nothing to improve my self-image. I'm ashamed to admit that I used words such as 'bastard' to his face. I did not even know what I was saying at times and, of course, there were occasions when I was sent out of class. Needless to say, I did not do well at French. My geography also suffered as Monsieur taught this subject too. He expected me to draw the maps he had set for homework, but this was something I found incredibly hard. Drawing was something I did with great difficulty. I grew to hate geography at school, although deep down I think I knew there was more to it. Nowadays, I find this subject challenging and exciting.

Maths was another subject I hated. I just could not do it. I found it boring and I wished it weren't considered such an important subject. My father was brilliant at maths and we spent many a *long* hour in the evening doing my maths homework. My maths teacher realised my difficulty, but at least we had an amicable relationship overall.

There were other subjects I enjoyed, such as English language and English literature. I was in my element writing essays and using my imagination. The downside of English was that I could not do a précis and, to this day, I still find this far from easy. Still, I excelled at history. I was good at learning dates and I found it interesting.

It was about this time I started writing my own stories. I had thoroughly enjoyed reading Enid Blyton for many years and now I was trying to write my own, albeit with a similar story line to hers. I also became an ardent reader of the comic '*June and School friend*' and started getting ideas from there. I loved books about horses too and used all this information for stimulation. I wanted to get my work published, but was not encouraged to do this by my parents. They saw what they believed to be the reality of the situation and that was I was highly unlikely to have my books accepted by any publisher. I felt dejected, squashed down and disappointed, but not surprised. After all, dreams don't come true for someone like me! Now as I remember these times in my life, I realise how we qualify things and so deprive ourselves of what the Lord may have in store for us. The enemy is so subtle: "*The thief comes only to steal and kill and destroy*" (*John 10:10*). My parents did buy me a book about publishing, but sadly I abandoned this idea completely. I decided the book looked boring and failed to investigate any of the information it put forward. I lacked the vision to pursue my dream. How many times do we give up, rather than tread the more uncertain, obscure way that leads to contentment and freedom? My school friends teased me about the books I read. I was twelve and still reading Enid Blyton.

I did well at sports. I was a good runner and often came second or third in the running race on sports day. I also enjoyed high jump and was proud of the fact I could jump about four feet at my best. I loved tennis too and pretended I would be a famous player one day. My imagination seemed to know no limits.

Time continued to elapse. I would soon have to face pastures new. I left Clark's College with two O-Levels: History and Religious Education. I was disappointed. I had expected to pass English, especially as I had passed my mock exam. I was also convinced I would pass my English Literature. The only compensation was that I had somehow passed Religious Education, despite giving it up for two years!

My parents had now decided I needed to become a proper young lady and a period away from home would prepare me for the future. I was to attend a finishing school, not in Switzerland (as was popular at the time), but somewhere in Britain. It had been my aunt's idea and my parents readily agreed.

I was sent to Bradbury House in Wiltshire, which is situated between Chippenham and Bath. I had never been away from home before for any length of time and suddenly the reality of the situation hit me with uncontrollable force. I felt vulnerable, afraid, with the security of home a distant dream. The tears flowed and I broke down the first night at the supper table in front of everyone.

Whilst I did make friends there, I was never truly happy. I longed for every Wednesday when we visited Bath, usually to go to the local cinema, or when we ventured out on a Saturday, normally to the same destination. We girls did go out for walks together that helped. We visited the famous theatre in Stratford-on-Avon and occasionally went on trips to places such as Bristol, Bradford-on-Avon and Lacock. I lived for the occasional visit from Mum and Dad, when they would take me out for a meal. I did re-take my English O-Levels whilst at Bradbury House, but once again failed to make the grade -- more ammunition for my overwhelming sense of failure. My parents wanted to keep me at Bradbury House another year, but I told them plainly how I felt. I can only say, to me, boarding school felt like prison and I longed to be free. In the end, we compromised. I stayed on another term and finally left school in December 1970.

I felt I was beginning again with my life. People try to tell you that school days are the best days of your life. I felt somewhat guilty that, for me, this just was not true. I was over the moon that at last it was all over, but I had yet to discover what lay ahead for me...

Chapter Two

Where do I go now?

As I finally left school, it was as if a big weight had been lifted! Yet, I had no idea of the way ahead. I was beginning a new chapter in my life, but the future seemed obscure and hidden. What path should I take? What direction should I go?

I had always been a dreamer, but making a career choice eluded me. I seemed to expect the job to come to me, instead of wholeheartedly investigating my options. Yet, not long after I left Bradbury House, my attention was forcibly turned away from me and on to my mother, who was beginning to experience heart problems. Her health was a constant source of worry to us as a family. Mum became a patient at the London Hospital Whitechapel for long periods of time, undergoing different tests to see how best to help her. Yet even in this period of darkness, I have many precious memories.

The journey from London to the remote location where we

lived was long and far, but nearly every day would find Dad and me on the now familiar route to visit Mum. I think the Lord used these occasions to draw my father and me closer together. We visited various restaurants and cafes. I enjoyed one Italian restaurant in particular and cannelloni became a firm favourite dish for me. I also recall travelling home after our trip to the hospital, trying to identify 'the mystery voice' on the radio. These were intimate special moments for us and will always be in my heart.

It was around this time I discovered I had a love of cooking. I was still at home, running the house whilst Mum was away. I especially relished making cheese dishes and unfamiliar deserts. I enjoyed experimenting with unusual ingredients and delving into old-fashioned cookery books, with the occasional more modern recipe book to satisfy the palate.

In April 1971, it was decided that in order for Mother to live a normal life, heart surgery was the best option. I believe it was by God's intervention and kindness that Mother eventually made a full physical recovery. We knew as a family that Mother's mother had suffered with heart trouble and other health problems for many years. Her late father had died of a cardiac arrest and her elder brother had suffered from heart disease all his life. Mother needed a coronary by-pass, as her coronary arteries were blocked. At the time this procedure was very much in its infancy and, unlike today, was a long and drawn out experience. My mother was in hospital for about ten weeks after surgery.

The future remained uncertain for me job-wise. I was eighteen and I still had no idea where I was going or what I wanted to do. I felt old and vulnerable. My father tried to get me a job at a local solicitor's office. I applied and failed, but I don't think I was too disappointed. Still the problem would not go away. What was I going to do with the rest of my life? Dad decided I had a natural love of cooking, so this was the path we decided to follow. I can see now he was doing what he felt was best for me, but to be honest there remained an element of doubt in my mind. Nevertheless in the September of 1971, I began a one year Hotel and Catering course about thirty miles away from home. I would lodge four nights a week in digs and travel half way home on the bus on Fridays, where my father would meet me. On Monday mornings he would drive me back to college and I would admire the beauty of the reservoir that we regularly passed.

I can't say these days were particularly happy for me, though. I was sensitive to the fact I was the eldest in my class and I wondered if I really was interested in making bread and cooking as a job. For a while, I consoled myself that I could be a hotel receptionist, but nothing seemed real. In addition, the people in my digs did not seem that friendly and I saw my time there as being strictly for sleeping purposes only. Eventually I did make friends. I started to go out to nightclubs in the evening and had two boyfriends. One was sixteen, which I saw as too young. The other was twenty-seven and too old, in my view.

Whilst at college, one of my friends invited me to an 'away' weekend, which involved the supernatural. I had no experience of such activities and in my naïvety asked Susanna if this was of Christian origin. She assured me the answer was no and I was left wondering what to do. I knew little or nothing of any religion apart from Christianity and, in one way, this meant a 'betrayal' of all that I believed. I decided it must be some kind of Eastern faith.

I attended the weekend meeting and found it fascinating. I now realise its roots were in the occult. Susanna agreed to be hypnotised and was able to access incidents when she was five years old. I was more cautious and did not wish to be out of my comfort zone. I did allow myself to be enticed by the sheer wonderment of it all, however. I was seen by a medium and the lady was able to tell me about my mother's dead parents. She also told me I had a love of history and advised me not to go into the nursing profession, (something I was not even thinking of at the time). I lapped up all this information eagerly and later, when I questioned my parents, I discovered what I had been told was true. Obviously, my love of history was undeniable. As I recall these events, I realise the good Lord was protecting me even then. Indeed, these had been forbidden practices when recorded in Scripture and could have opened the door for me to be drawn into some very dangerous works of the enemy, namely Satan himself.

I completed the Hotel and Catering course in July 1972, but shuddered at the thought of putting into practice all I had learnt at college. I allowed myself to succumb to my fears; instead of facing them head on... remaining in limbo as I refused to confront my confidence problems. I left college the day after getting drunk on my nineteenth birthday, waking up to a blinding headache and vomiting. Hardly a decorous way to leave my digs accommodation and not the parting I would have wished for. I look back on that particular birthday with mixed emotions. I have only been drunk once in my life and that was that particular birthday night, when I had deliberately set out to be so. Having previously been so protected by my family, that night I indulged in escapism. I was also having women's health troubles at that time, so my parents had kindly arranged for me to see a gynaecologist privately on our way home from college. Still suffering from the effects of the night before, I longed instead to go to my parents' home and relax. Nevertheless the specialist did reassure me. I was relieved he felt I would still be able to bear children, despite my current problems.

It was becoming clear that I could not pursue this work avoidance forever. I thought of being an air stewardess, working on a ship, or being an au pair, but everything seemed a fantasy. I loved the idea of travelling and seeing the world, but I also remained a home-loving girl. I even mentioned becoming a farm secretary to my father, but this was not welcomed or encouraged.

I then started working in the local geriatric hospital as a cleaner. I did this for about three months and decided to try my hand at what was known at the time as auxiliary nursing, which I did for about a year. The job consisted of looking after the elderly, seeing to their basic needs. It was a real eye opener to me. I was suddenly confronted with the reality of caring for incontinent patients, and all the unpleasantness associated with it. My heart went out to the residents suffering from dementia and I wondered what they had been like when they had been well. Eventually I moved from my parents' address into the Nurses' Home. It was there I met Frances, my future sister-in-law, Amelia, my friend from Great Yarmouth, and some very friendly Filipino girls. Some of the girls there were doing their student or pupil training and weren't much older than myself. I was relatively happy at this time, but I still had that inner desire for more. I was determined to prove myself to my family, so I decided to train as a nurse. I wonder now if I was really doing it out of pride rather than for the right reasons.

Around this time my Dad decided to treat me to some contact lenses for my twentieth birthday. I adapted to them well and soon became confident and happy wearing them.

My brother Paul and I went on holiday around various parts of England in the summer of 1973. We travelled to the Chilterns, the Cotswolds, the Peak district and the counties of Shropshire and Herefordshire. We visited well-known historic houses such as Chatsworth House and Blenheim Palace. We enjoyed exploring the famous university cities of Oxford and Cambridge.

I recall how ridiculously superstitious I was. I managed to break a face mirror in the car and promptly broke into tears, convinced of being doomed to seven years bad luck. Oh the chains that bound me! Paul tried to console me, but to no avail.

When I arrived home I was in for shock! I knew I had eaten well, but surely not that well? I weighed ten stone! I couldn't believe it. It was then that Paul confessed that he had put the scales 'on' a stone for me, thereby giving me the shock of my life!

These are happy memories as I reminisce, but was the decision to start my nursing training based on some romantic 'Mills and Boon' nursing fairy-tale, 'pie in the sky' escape from reality? I found attending the School of Nursing training a challenge in itself. Taking a person's blood pressure did not come naturally to me or to another girl in the group. But, 'practice makes perfect' and I struggled on because I had no desire to be seen as a failure. At least initially we were home every weekend, but that soon finished when we started working on the wards.

I found nursing on the ward far removed from what I had imagined it to be. I didn't like some of the jobs we had to do, such as giving out bedpans, changing incontinent patients, replacing dirty dressings, taking temperatures etc. I still lacked confidence and why I continued in this profession is a mystery to me.

I had only been nursing for three months when I was struck down by a severe form of tonsillitis and was forced to have my first working Christmas off. My parents were away skiing, so I spent that Christmas with my Auntie Sheila and Uncle Gerald.

I returned to work with little enthusiasm about two weeks later. I had only been back at work a few days when I received an unexpected letter in the post. I read it while sitting in the hospital canteen and was shocked to learn of my Grandmother's death. I could scarcely take it in. I had seen Grandma very recently, whilst staying at my aunt's. She had been well and very much her normal self. It was later I discovered that Grandma had suffered a major stroke whilst out shopping. I felt devastated and in a complete state of shock. I was to see the 'good side' of human nature that afternoon, but also sadly the darker side. I returned to the ward and the Sister on duty was a brick. She told me to go off duty and try and cheer myself up. I met a nursing friend, Wanda Smith, who was in my class. She invited me to go out with her and her boyfriend. I agreed and, as predicted, felt better in myself. Sometime later, I learnt from Wanda's aunt (who was to become a good friend) that Wanda's boyfriend had stolen some money from me that night when I had been in a particularly vulnerable frame of mind. The Lord in his goodness had hidden this episode from me.

Time passed and I was now approaching the grand old age of twenty-one. I had had several boyfriends by now, but I cannot recall who my main man-friend was at that age. I was reunited with Frances, who I knew from our previous work experience at the local geriatric hospital. She was in the nursing cohort behind me, but her passion for her work was very obvious. The two of us continued to develop a close friendship with each other.

I was determined to celebrate my twenty-first birthday in style, so a big party and a disco were arranged. We had a marquee on the lawn, dancing, lots of noise, and great fun. I enjoyed seeing people I had not seen for a while, which included lost friends from school and distant acquaintances from the past. I felt important and enjoyed being the centre of attention. The party finished about four o'clock in the morning. It was amazingly generous of my father to present me with such happy memories to treasure, and it was only many years later that I realised what a tremendous financial cost it had been to him personally. At the time I took it all for granted.

It was shortly after this that a nursing friend and I went on holiday together. Catherine, as I will call her, was a girl with whom I could empathise. We had previously gone youth hostelling in Scotland. That was the first time that I had been introduced to a rucksack and I had hated it. Would I ever get used to carrying heavy baggage on my back? Somehow, I didn't think so. In those days hostellers were denied the comparative luxury they have today -- no cars were allowed and hostellers had certain duties to perform before they were permitted to escape the clutches of their accommodation. We had visited Stirling, Edinburgh and its famous sites, and the Trossachs. This holiday we travelled abroad on a cruise, flying to Portugal and from there to Madeira, a beautiful picturesque island consisting of hills and mountains, with flowers everywhere. Our journey continued to some of the Canary Islands, where Lanzarote in particular struck me as being very different. Parts of it felt as if we had arrived on the moon!

Soon after this holiday, as part of my training, I was moved to another hospital, which focused mainly on geriatrics and outpatients. It was while I was there that I became very aware of a Christian witness at the Nurses Home where I was living. I sensed that I was going nowhere in life, just plodding along and hoping for the best. There had to be more to life than this. I wanted what these other people had. I also recognised my need of forgiveness as a sinner. I longed for the reassurance that I was going to heaven if I died, so it was not entirely without selfish motives that I invited Jesus Christ into my life. My Christian friends were there for me, as we prayed together. Life took a new direction and would never be the same again.

Chapter Three

New Found Faith

I now felt wrapped up and cocooned in a form of paradise. I was one of comparatively few Christians who had experienced salvation and baptism in the spirit simultaneously. I felt a sense of joy and laughter, especially when I was in the presence of my new Christian friends. This sadly didn't cross over into my working life. I felt somewhat embarrassed when shortly after this I met a lady, who, as an eye specialist, had tested my eyes many years ago when I was a child. Here we were, together once more, and this time I was a pupil nurse. The whole thing seemed very bizarre. I wonder now why I allowed myself to feel this way. We have choices in life and I rather unwisely succumbed to pride, alongside my feelings of inadequacy.

However, at this time the most meaningful part of my life was my newfound faith. I treasured the meetings we held together in Samantha and James' home. I loved the choruses we sang, such as '*In the name of Jesus we have the victory*'.

I longed to know about Christianity and often questioned, in great detail, the reason why the believers were so committed to serving Jesus. I also valued the informality of coming together and using the gift of tongues, something I had never heard of before.

I became more determined to follow Christ wholeheartedly and when baptism was suggested, Helen, a nursing colleague, and I readily consented to it. I did wonder if I was agreeing to this idea too soon, as most people tend to wait a while longer. Yet, I have since found out that it is probably more biblical to be baptised as soon as possible after conversion.

As the new year of 1975 dawned, I did something different. I stayed up, and welcomed the incoming year, at church. It made the year 'extra special' and made Christ very real to me.

In January that year, Helen and I were baptised by being fully immersed in water. I was disappointed that my parents were not there to witness this event. I had been christened as a baby and they may well have considered adult baptism to be totally unnecessary. They would have had to travel a considerable distance, which might also have been a factor. But, my parents ventured to say they felt I had been 'brain washed' and that what happened to me would not last. How good it is to know their predictions did not materialise. I am still going on, 'strong' in the Lord, all these years later.

There was one middle aged Christian lady in our fellowship group whom I especially remember. Emma Joyce literally radiated joy. Now as I think back, I wonder, was it the joy of the Lord, or was she a bubbly character anyway? I like to think it was the former. I have never known anyone else quite like her.

When we could, Helen and I attended a 'well known' vicar's church several miles away. People were healed there and healing seemed to be the 'norm'. I lapped it up with the simplistic faith of a child. I was well at the time, so it never crossed my mind that God might not heal. As I saw it, that was part of his goodness.

Time, of course, never stands still and I returned to the main hospital once more. I missed the Christian fellowship I had become accustomed to. I no longer attended a church and nothing seemed the same. I wish someone had told me the importance of reading and studying the Word because, as far as I recall, this was never mentioned and I therefore fell back into some of my old habits of wrongful thinking.

I would like to mention Wanda Smith's aunt once more, as it has been my privilege to know her. She was a lady named Helen Robinson and a committed Christian. Sometime later, I met Helen's parents, the Johnsons -- a couple who obviously loved the Lord. They lived some distance away from the hospital, but were a great encouragement to me with their warm personalities and the various books they shared on their faith. I have my misgivings as to whether I would have remained in the faith, but for these dear dedicated followers of the Lord. They even made arrangements for me to visit some much nearer Christians, closer to where I was currently living.

In spite of having found some Christian fellowship, I was not happy in my work. I continued to persevere, though, to prove my worth. The job did not satisfy and I constantly seemed to be struggling. It was then that a nurse I vaguely knew said she was planning to do her psychiatric training. This made me stop and listen. I questioned myself. Was this what I wanted to do? I could see myself in this work. Ordinary nursing had lost any appeal and I longed for something different. I thought about this, but I regret to say I did not pray, as far as I remember. I shared my desires with my parents, but they were far from supportive. They considered my ideas to be outlandish and not something their well-educated daughter should be undertaking. I felt angry and disappointed. Why were my suggestions cast aside? I was determined to eventually do what was in my heart and stuck to my principles.

I completed my general nurse training around December 1975. I was relieved it was over and looked forward hopefully to venturing into pastures new. I was placed on a geriatric ward doing night work and I remained there for about six months.

I decided to take a break from nursing altogether for the summer of 1976. I wanted to see more of Scotland and applied for a job on the island of Mull. I worked in a kitchen doing menial tasks. The work was hard and the wages poor, but the scenery was beautiful and very different to what I was used to. The weather was the only disappointment, as it rained a great deal. I found this hard to accept, when the weather in England was so warm, and settled that summer. We had coach parties and ordinary tourists to entertain. My mother came to visit me for a week, so I didn't feel quite so alone.

She was staying on the mainland at Oban, and travelled over on the ferry to see me.

The island of Iona was next door and I relished the opportunity to visit the Abbey there, which is steeped in Christian tradition. The atmosphere was majestic and serene. It seemed to possess a unique sense of peace and holiness, possibly gathered from the accumulated prayers of the saints throughout the centuries. I visited Iona on several occasions.

In August, Scotland too had a period of hot dry weather that I particularly welcomed. I nearly travelled to Fort William one day, but decided the risk of not catching the last ferry back to Mull on time was just too great. It was with a tinge of sadness, and regret, that I left Mull. I returned to England in early September. I had managed to attend regular church services during this time, but they lacked the enthusiasm I had thrived on when I first knew the Lord.

October came, and with it yet another opportunity to spread my wings. I was excited and nervous. I was away from home and once more found myself facing an unknown and mysterious future. What would this new career, psychiatric nursing, bring? Would I finally find what I had been looking for all along, or would I be disappointed yet again?

Chapter Four

New beginnings

Again, I found myself immersed in an altogether different world. I was a new girl once more and found myself feeling lost and alone. I especially felt disappointed that Frances, my future sister-in-law, had made the decision to leave psychiatric nursing, before I came, and return once again to general nursing. It would mean starting afresh and making new friends. Yet it was not to be too long before I met Celia and formed a good relationship with her. Celia was in a different group to me, training to become a psychiatric registered nurse. I had decided to remain an enrolled nurse. My course was to be only for a year, due to my previous nursing experience. We have been friends ever since.

I found I enjoyed the course. I was very interested, and fascinated, by mental illness and especially intrigued as to why some individuals appeared to be more predisposed to this sickness than others. Schizophrenia often seemed to be in the genes and my heart went out to families affected by this unwelcome affliction.

I started on the admission ward, which I especially enjoyed. Many of my patients were suffering from post-natal depression. They were encouraged to have their babies with them and given as much support as they needed to regain their confidence. In time, it was hoped they would make a full recovery.

Some young girls there were suffering from anorexia. This was difficult for me to understand. Why would they not just eat? I was someone who loved my food, so this disassociation with it was bizarre to me. In the 1970's so little was known about anorexia and it is only in recent years that the cause of this awful illness has been more properly recognised.

These were the days of ECT (electro-convulsive therapy), where patients were given an epileptic shock after receiving an injection to induce sleep. Just how these treatments worked I don't know, but they were meant to help people with depression. One of the side effects, however, was memory loss.

Some of these patients were sectioned, as they were considered to be a danger to other people, or possibly at risk of self- harm. Most of the clients, however, were informal and could come and go as they pleased.

There were yet other patients who had what was then known as 'manic depression' (now called bipolar disorder). The manic side of this condition is where the patient can seem to have unlimited bouts of energy, spend impulsively, have little or no sleep and do the oddest things. The opposite side of this condition is a terrible depression, where there seems to be no way out. Treatment is to get the individual back to a normal level, so that they are seen as being neither too high nor too low. This usually involves tablets to correct the bio-chemical balance in the brain.

It was at this time I noticed that many of the nurses were foreign in origin, often coming from countries such as Malaysia and Hong-Kong. Unlike in general nursing, many psychiatric nurses were male.

There was one particular ward that was known as the 'locked ward'. These were the days when patients were still 'locked up' for safety. Strong tranquillisers administered by injection were often given to calm the resident down. Many of the individuals were long-term clients. We did occasionally have murderers placed there. I often wondered what had led some of these people to become so deranged.

Around this time, I started to have trouble with my eyes. I no longer found contact lenses comfortable to wear, but was advised not to wear my glasses because they were likely to be broken by the patients. I was fortunate whilst I was there, though. I was never injured or attacked, but think with hindsight that the Good Lord was looking after me. As trainee nurses, we were all expected to work on night duty and it was on this particular 'locked' ward that my night duty began.

After I had been on this course for about ten months I arranged to go on a Christian holiday, based in the Peak District. I travelled up with my friends who were considerably older than me, apart from one young man who seemed to be on his own.

It was certainly a different holiday than I was used to. The accommodation was very basic and reminded me of boarding school dormitories. The men were on their side and us women on ours. It was quite an eye opener for someone accustomed to modern day comforts.

The messages were interesting and challenging, but for me a little on the longwinded side. I found services of three hours or longer hard to digest and welcomed the finish.

I also felt disappointed with the weather that year. Unlike the previous summer, the weather was wet and miserable and hardly ideal for walking. I felt 'let down' by the Lord. Why hadn't He given us decent weather? I thought it was unfair. Just why I felt the Lord should favour me I don't know. I was young, selfish and wanting my own way.

I continued to notice that this young man, whose name was Paul, often sat alone and my heart, went out to him. He was painfully shy and I longed to reassure him. I spoke to him and invited myself to sit with him. We became closer and gradually more at ease with each other.

Paul drove me to the nearby towns of Chesterfield and Buxton. One day we ventured further than we had intended and to our surprise we realised we were on the outskirts of Sheffield. We had seen a little of the beauty of the Peak District.

After the holiday, some of the intense Christian learning I had so recently received began to recede. I was once again drawn into the darkness and deception of this dark world. I became briefly attracted to some of the male nurses working at the hospital, one in particular. Thankfully the Lord used my conscience to stop me from going any further with this relationship. I am so thankful to the Johnsons and Helen for assuring me that such a move would be totally wrong in the Lord's sight. I wanted to justify how I felt, but I knew the case was totally against the Lord's will. It is clear in Scripture that a Christian and a non-believer are not to come together in the union of a marriage, and who was I to violate God's Word? It says in the second letter to the Corinthians, *"What does a believer have in common with an unbeliever? What agreement is there between the temple of God and idols? For we are the temple of the living God"* (*2 Corinthians 6:15b-16a*). I reluctantly agreed to end the relationship. The enemy can be so subtle. Yes, the Lord had his hand on my life. I was still dating Paul and broke his heart, something to this day I am deeply ashamed about.

As time passed, I was able to see more clearly that being married to this man was not God's plan for me.

Paul was quiet and gentle and extremely patient. I had infatuation. He had love. We began to take each other seriously and, in March 1978, Paul and I were engaged.

It was also at this time that I had an opportunity to visit Israel. My mother had hoped to be my companion, but unfortunately was not well enough to accompany me, so Frances stepped in. Paul was also unable to make the trip, but had been to Israel several years before. I could not believe we were in Israel! It seemed like some far off dream. I was in the land where Jesus our Lord walked. I loved the experience. It seemed exquisite, out of this world.

I enjoyed going to the biblical sites, but about one third

of the time I was afflicted with a tummy bug that meant a few disappointments. For instance, I missed seeing the church of the Holy Sepulchre, but fortunately was very privileged to visit the garden of Gethsemane and look at the open tomb. The atmosphere was something special. There was a sense of God's glory, of His awesome beauty and presence. There was something unique and altogether different about the whole place.

We also travelled to the Sea of Galilee. It reminded me of Lake Geneva in Switzerland. The scenery, the hills, all had a story to tell. I could imagine our Lord fishing there with his disciples, speaking his parables, and appealing for people to live this way because He loved them and knew what was best for them.

Capernaum, though, was a disappointment to me. It was a city of ruins. Now I think I would appreciate its beauty and remoteness more than I did back then.

There was still danger and terrorist activity happening in 1978 and just before my holiday party returned to the United Kingdom there was an attack on a bus, which involved loss of life. I could not wait to escape from Israel. I felt frightened and vulnerable.

When we finally arrived back in England I was exhausted. I knew I could not face working the next day. I was just too tired. I managed to change my shifts and start later in the week.

Spring turned into summer. My brother's marriage to Frances was to be in July and I was to be one of the bridesmaids. Their wedding ceremony was to be in a quiet country location. The church was situated not far from the farm where we had grown up. It was heartening to know that just two months later it would be my turn. Having treated me to a big occasion on my twenty-first birthday, Dad seemed reluctant to repeat his generosity to me a second time. I felt saddened by this and found it difficult to accept. I wondered if the fact that Paul came from a working class background rather than a middle class background was the reason? Only the Lord knows our hearts and possibly I was totally out of order for entertaining these thoughts.

September 30th finally came. I could not believe what was happening. The weather was cold, with threatening rain, and an unpleasant chilly wind. This time Frances and Paul's younger sister, Helen, were bridesmaids.

My Uncle Charles helped us to choose some of our hymns. Paul liked the hymn '*Great is thy faithfulness.*' I was determined to have the good old familiar wedding tune that introduces the bride and groom's forthcoming union. We both had rings that were blessed.

I was privileged to have the reception in a marquee situated on the farm lawn. It was a very nostalgic setting.

When it was time to go, Paul's friends of many years drove us away to their local village. We had the sign on the back of the car that displayed, '*Just Married*' on it and cans at the rear of the vehicle, highlighting the occasion. I was proud to be Paul's wife.

We spent the first night of our honeymoon at a hotel in Huntingdon, before slowly making our way northwards to Scotland. We passed by the romantic location of Gretna

Green, where years ago couples ran away to wed, and can still do so today. We travelled up the east side of Scotland to John O'Groats. I enjoyed seeing Ullapool and proudly showing off my shiny new wedding ring to the other interested hotel guests.

Aviemore was another must. It had certainly changed from the quiet remote village that my Dad, brother and Diane had visited in the 1960's. Now it was more built up and an obvious commercial tourist spot. We settled on a Bed and Breakfast to stay in. It was cold and we asked if we could have the central heating on. This was not granted, rather to our disappointment.

On one occasion the road we were travelling on was so severely flooded that people had to be rescued by helicopter. Yet it was not all doom and gloom. There was to be a final fling of what one would call an Indian summer as Paul and I ascended Ben Nevis on a hot October day. The sun shone brightly and it was good to view this well-known mountain in all its majestic glory.

After our climb, we attempted to drive home, all the way from northern Scotland, in one day. In the end we succumbed to tiredness and spent the night in a Northampton hotel. So near and yet so far!

Time passed, we settled into married life. I continued to work in the psychiatric hospital and Paul remained working in his soft drinks factory.

I was thankful when I was moved from the 'sick ward' to another 'long term' ward, with patients who were chronically ill. This was more where I felt I wanted to be. Of course people can't help being physically ill, but this was not why I had come into psychiatric nursing. The nursing sister was lovely and very kind and I felt reasonably content. Sometime later I was moved yet again to a ward on my own. I did not like my own company and initially wondered how I would cope, but I became accustomed to the new environment. I found some of the patients had challenging issues and I enjoyed getting to know them and their stories.

It was now about three years since my marriage to Paul and we felt the time had come to try for a baby. As I had feared, it was not easy. My periods were irregular and I therefore did not know when I was ovulating. Paul was tested too, to check for infertility. Eventually, after seeing the doctor, I was referred to the gynaecologist and placed on fertility treatment. Soon after this I became pregnant and remained in my job until seven months into my pregnancy. I was ecstatic and over the moon. Yet Paul and I were to face an unimaginable pain we could never have anticipated.

Chapter Five

Matthew

How were Paul and I to know that all the planning, all the expectation of a newborn baby would, in the end, result in an unbearable heartache? Only those afflicted by such anguish can truly understand just what it means to have nothing at the end of a pregnancy. I had been so excited. I had longed for a baby for two years. The period of waiting had seemed like an eternity, but finally it had happened.

Eventually, there I was aged thirty and expecting our first baby. I was over the moon. How could I know that our hopes were going to be dashed a mere thirty-six hours after our child's birth? As soon as our son was born, he was rushed to the special care unit. He was so sick and frail.

The pregnancy had seemed almost perfect, until near the end. The only problem, as far as I was concerned, was that I was so small. I hardly looked pregnant at nearly nine months and, unlike most would-be mothers, I wanted everyone to know I was expecting. But this was just not the case.

Nevertheless, I was very happy and excited. I had sailed through the pregnancy, unlike some, with no morning sickness and no toxaemia. Frances was expecting her first baby too and was due about two weeks before me. Everything seemed just fine until I saw my consultant, Mr Harrison, one morning for a routine check-up.

"You'll have to come in," he said. I paused, amazed.

"Why?" I questioned.

"Because your oestrogen levels are too low," he answered. "Your placenta isn't functioning properly and we are concerned at your lack of weight. I want you to come in this afternoon."

I guess I should have been prepared for something like this, but I wasn't.

I went home and rang my husband and then my Mum and Dad. Paul worked in Oxbury, over twenty miles away from our home in Endlesham near Twinmere. It was awkward for him to come home and take me into hospital from such a distance. My parents, though not strictly retired, were their own bosses and had more time to help out, so they were able to take me to hospital instead. I was weepy, emotional and upset because of the unforeseen problems.

We arrived at the hospital sometime during that same afternoon. I had three weeks to go before the baby was due. I wondered how I would spend all that time in hospital?

Paul came to see me on the antenatal ward that evening. I can't remember now, but just having him there must have been a source of comfort and strength to me. Paul is a quiet, shy person who tends to keep his thoughts and feelings to himself, but he can be very kind, and very protective, to people who are especially vulnerable. This included his mother. Paul is very sensitive, but when used wisely sensitivity can be a precious jewel.

I quickly settled in and became accustomed to the rather monotonous routine. I found being plugged into the monitor that recorded the baby's heartbeat especially fascinating. Every time I felt the baby kick I had to press a button. Our baby was sluggish compared to others -- he or she didn't move much. I can't say it did not worry me, it did. Why didn't our baby move like other babies? The nurses did the best they could to reassure me.

Another thing that fascinated me was the baby's heartbeat. A baby's heart pulsates much quicker than an adult's. An infant heart beats on average between 120-170 beats per minute. A tendency for the heart rate to be between 110 - 140 beats per minute can indicate a boy and over 140 beats a minute, a girl. The monitor seemed to suggest a boy and in some way I was disappointed.

Every morning we were routinely tested. My results were mostly normal, although earlier in my pregnancy sugar had been found to be present in my urine, a problem that is fairly common in expectant mums. My blood pressure remained high, but it was better than it had been.

The other patients at the time were a great inspiration to me. One lady was expecting twins. She already had three children and her second child had Down's syndrome. How did she cope? One handicapped child, as well as other children, and the sadness of knowing her little boy was different and, with the exception of a miracle, would never be normal. Apart from God's intervention, I could not explain or understand her casual attitude, her total acceptance of the situation. It is ironic, as I look back now, for I too was to experience a similar pain and burden, just as heartrending as this mother's.

Then there was Chris, a likable bubbly young woman who already had one young child and was expecting another. Chris was in hospital because she had high blood pressure and toxaemia.

While I was in hospital, I heard that Frances had had her baby -- a boy named Michael. It had proved to be a difficult birth and she had needed to have a forceps delivery. I was happy for her and my brother and also glad for my parents. Michael was their first grandchild. What a coincidence that Frances and I had been pregnant together, our babies due within days of each other. I wished in my heart it was over for me too.

Frances has a strong character. She is one of four children and her parents divorced when her youngest sister, Amanda, was around nine years old. Frances's mother had left Amanda to be brought up by their father. Frances comes across as being a very practical, confident and kind person who cares enough to sometimes say things other people would rather not hear. Sadly Frances has no contact with her mother.

I wanted so much for it to be our turn soon and for all this waiting in hospital to be worth it! Yet there was caution too. What if something went wrong? I told myself not to be silly, that I'd been there a while and still had some time to go. God was not going to let me down, especially as I'd had to wait all that time. But, looking back was God trying to prepare me for what lay ahead and I did not want to know?

There was another lady on the ward, my current roommate, whose name was Annette. She had been trying for a baby for five years. It made my two years look like nothing. Annette had been warned that her baby might have a cleft palate. She herself suffered from Crohn's disease and, as a result, had needed much medication throughout her pregnancy, which was not ideal. Her problems far outweighed mine.

One of the nurses at the time made a strong impression on me. Her name was Joanna and she was not one of the regular ward nurses. Joanna was a born again Christian, a mother of four and working part time at the Maternity Hospital. I can't remember all she said just now, but I found her to be homely and pleasant and a true mother figure. She went to a lively Anglican Church. I missed her when she wasn't on duty.

One Sunday, before the baby was due, I asked and received permission to go out for the afternoon. I was extremely happy and grateful to be away from ward routine for a while. The baby was very active that afternoon and I felt the joy of him kicking me, which only a mother-to-be can truly sense. It was a lovely day.

Soon after my return to hospital, there was talk of me having a Caesarean section, because my pelvis was too small. The thought filled me with sorrow. I did not want to be unconscious when the baby was born. I wanted a normal birth, thank you very much!

I shared this with my Pastor and we prayed. I was keen that God would have His way. I was very thankful and relieved when my consultant said that I could have the baby normally. What a relief!

About two days before the baby was due to be born, according to my dates, I was informed that, in the interests of safety to the unborn child, I was to be induced. Such a disappointment! I had wanted the baby to be born naturally, but both my husband and I agreed that the doctors knew what they were doing. It was Wednesday morning and I was given a pessary to induce labour. By evening it was obvious that it wasn't working and I was given another one. This time the effect was quite dramatic and a few hours later I was in a great deal of pain. Paul did his best to reassure me while I walked up and down the ward corridor, in what felt like agony. Yet, although it was obvious to my husband and me at the time, none of the staff seemed to believe that I was in labour and we were left to our own devices.

I remember one nurse, who must have been near to retirement, telling me to relax. She told me I was far too tense and that was why the pain was so bad.

My husband had to go home, having been warned that he might be called back sometime in the night. I guess I must have fallen asleep, but this is faint in my memory. It was during the night that my waters burst and I was rushed to the delivery room. Paul arrived about half an hour later, which seemed an age to me.

"You're not pushing right," voiced the nurse.

I kept trying to praise the Lord silently, through the pain, whilst thinking to myself, "If this is having a baby, forget it. I can't bear it. It's worse than I imagined. How can people put up with this pain time after time?" It was totally beyond me.

There were problems. I heard the nurse's voice again, "We'll have to call the duty doctor." This was quite commonplace and I wasn't unduly concerned. It was quite reassuring to have a doctor there. Yet, nothing changed straight away.

It became more and more apparent that I was not pushing 'right' and that something would have to be done. Guilt had started to envelop me. Why couldn't I be like the mothers on films who always pushed so well?

"You need a forceps delivery," advised the doctor. I was relieved -- at last something was being done to get the baby out.

"I can't take this pain much longer," I gasped.

It still seemed an age before the baby was born, but finally it was all over. I knew immediately that something was wrong. The baby had not screamed and my husband and I had not been given him to hold in our arms.

After being told we had a girl, we were informed we had a boy. I was sick after the birth and tried to settle back with my husband and relax. Paul went to find out what was wrong. The baby was very ill.

We were informed that he had had serious breathing difficulties and had been on a ventilator. He was off it now, though, and holding his own.

I was stunned. I prayed to the Lord for him to be alright. I don't think we had really taken in just how ill he was. I reasoned with myself that many babies were very ill when they were first born, but they recovered. Surely our boy, who we named Matthew, would be the same as others before him? He wouldn't be any different... would he?

Paul went home and I was left to my thoughts. I longed to see Matthew, but had to wait. After some rest, I was taken to see the baby in the Special Care Baby Unit. What I saw shocked me! He was back on the ventilator. Numerous tubes surrounded him. Even though I am an ex-nurse, seeing him like this scared the life out of me. He looked so poorly, so helpless, and there was nothing I could do to change the situation. It was awful to witness. No one could do anything and I was trapped in this nightmare.

I can't remember what time Paul returned, but he had time off work. He too was surprised when he saw Matthew.

"I thought he was alright," he gasped. "I've even opened a Post Office Savings Account for him!"

"Don't you think that's a bit premature?" I replied, "After all he's very ill."

Yet, neither of us realised just how ill he was. I guess we didn't want to know. It was all too awful, all too horrific.

There was a lovely born again nursing sister, Margaret Fisher, who was working in the Special Care Baby Unit at this time. I had known her previously when we had both attended Christian meetings up at the General Hospital. It was so good to have someone there who I knew personally. Margaret was a tower of strength to me. I knew she cared. She would do her best to make sure Matthew survived.

"If you like, you can cuddle the baby", she said.

These words should have given me hope and comfort, but

right then I was not ready.

"No, it's alright," I replied, feeling somewhat uncomfortable.

The truth was that I lacked the confidence, and courage, to hold baby Matthew. I could not adjust to seeing our child surrounded by endless tubes and holding him may have unnerved me still further. Paul was content to follow my example.

I look back now with sadness and regret. Why didn't I hold Matthew, instead of giving in to fear? I would urge you, if you are ever in a similar position, to yield to your maternal instincts and cuddle your child.

We sat by Matthew's bedside for what seemed an age. We took turns to hold his hands as a way of showing that we loved him.

I remember the delight I felt when Matthew seemed to respond to our attention. His eyes were firmly shut and his reflexes were not working, but there seemed to be a slight movement in one foot. This tiny sign was a huge comfort to us.

"Matthew is trying to tell us he wants to get better," I thought. "He knows we want so much for him to recover."

Of course, the hospital staff differed from us in how they saw the situation and patiently explained there were other reasons for him moving his foot, but I wanted my own version then. It meant so much to Paul and me.

I have to confess that, to my shame, my first impressions of Matthew's appearance had been less than delighted. I noticed he hardly had any hair, his ears stuck out, and he was far from handsome. How could I have been so prideful as to allow these thoughts to go through my mind? But, as soon as I realised just how ill he was, these feelings were put in check. All that really mattered was that Matthew came through this ordeal without permanent ill effects.

I cannot recall everything very clearly now. It is many years since Matthew's birth and, for some unknown reason; I stopped writing my faithful diary at this time. Yet I do remember that I was very physically frail and weak -- my forceps delivery had left me very sore. It was because of this that I had to be wheeled from the ward to the Special Care Baby Unit, as I was not strong enough to walk there myself without help. All I remember is rest, sleep and seeing baby Matthew.

Paul and I, as followers of Jesus, believed in the power of prayer and healing. I knew that God could heal Matthew and make him well. I was certain prayer could change things! We informed many of our Christian friends that Matthew had been born and that he was very ill. I don't know whether we had said 'critically ill' but I am sure they received the message and understood. Not caring about the cost, we even rang Paul's Christian friends in Germany. As I have already said, I do strongly believe in the power of prayer. We thought that the greater the number of people praying for our baby, the better the chance he would have to recover. I wonder what other people think about this.

I kept on pondering the words of *Psalm 56 v 3*, '*When I am afraid, I will trust in you*'. I thought the Lord was testing our faith and would bring us through. He knew how much we wanted this baby. I really failed to see, at the time, that what really mattered was what God wanted, and not what we felt was our right. Despite the intercession for Matthew, he failed to improve. I questioned if it was a lack of faith on our part -- if we had believed more, would it have been different?

I stepped away from Matthew for a short time and returned to find the medical staff resuscitating him. This happened several times in his short life. It was like some horrific dream, but as if the nightmare were happening to someone else. We could not face up to reality or admit the truth.

Matthew was now fifteen hours old. It was evening and Margaret advised us that if we wanted Matthew dedicated, it had to be done immediately. The next day may be too late.

I managed to telephone Pastor Terry Bates, the minister of our Assemblies of God (AoG) church. He was out for the evening, but his sixteen year-old daughter, Hannah, promised to tell him the news on his return. This was a relief as I was very tired by this time. We both had had a long day and, in addition to the stress, I had gone through a difficult labour. Looking back, I am convinced that the Lord gave me the will, and the stamina, to wait and witness Matthew's dedication.

I remember Paul and I discussing healing with the pastor and his wife, Linda. I recall saying we should pray, 'If it be Thy will, heal Matthew!' but Pastor Terry said that that wasn't necessary and that I need not concern myself with this statement.

I was quite happy to agree with the pastor. After all, Paul and I were still in shock and unable to contest anything. The pastor dedicated Matthew to the Lord. It was a relief to know that, if anything happened to the baby, at least he was dedicated; even though I am sure the Lord would have been merciful to him.

When everyone went home, I returned to the ward. I cannot recall my thoughts that night. I guess I must have been sedated, for I vaguely remember waking up next morning to the on-going nightmare. A kind nurse came to my bedside with a photo of the baby in her hand.

"How is Matthew?" I inquired.

"He is holding his own," she replied.

"At least he isn't dead," I thought.

It seemed to me that night time was somehow the worst time of all. The fact that Matthew had survived another night gave me some hope. I looked at the photo again.

"How helpless our baby looks," I thought. "If only, if only…"

Those tubes everywhere bothered me. Even though the ventilator and life-saving equipment was keeping him alive, they revolted me.

It was still quite early in the morning when I broke down in tears and sobbed my heart out. Our baby was so very ill and all around me there were other mothers sitting with their healthy babies. It was too much for me. A young woman, aged about nineteen, came up to me and began to speak. Her baby was in the Special Care Baby Unit. She was not upset. I believe she realised that her baby was in the best place. Her child would be in the Intensive Care Unit until it was considered well enough to be in a normal ward. I did feel slightly comforted by her and I am grateful to her for trying to help me. But I knew there was something terribly wrong with Matthew. He seemed different from all the other babies in the unit.

It should have been such a happy day. It was September 30th, and our fifth Wedding Anniversary. It was one of the dates that I had been given to expect Matthew. We received a congratulations card for Matthew -- the sender had not known how ill he was. We had two anniversary cards.

"What a day!" I thought. "Surely the Lord won't let Matthew be taken today. After all, it is our anniversary. Please spare him until at least tomorrow," I prayed.

When Paul arrived I showed him the photo and I think he felt like me about it. Matthew seemed about the same when we saw him. Doctors spoke to us about him, but we were unable to grasp the full facts.

Margaret called Paul and I aside to speak with us privately. As we sipped coffee she explained that Matthew was very ill and we should be prepared for the worst.

"But" I responded, "We're praying for him and our friends are also praying. I know he is very ill, but God can heal him."

"But He doesn't always," Margaret replied tenderly, "Sometimes it isn't His way."

I sat there dumbfounded. We did not really want to hear. We wanted a happy ending. After all, we'd been trying for two long years for this baby. Yet, in my heart, I couldn't help wondering if Margaret was right.

Later, when I was alone in my bed, the family G.P. came in to visit me. Dr. Emerson was kind and sympathetic, but also honest and truthful. He explained that if Matthew survived, he would be seriously brain damaged.

Our child would be like a cabbage. I squirmed. I could

scarcely take it in. I was devastated. I could not understand how this could be. What had gone wrong? Surely the Lord could heal him even of this horrific brain damage? We shared the news with other Christians and they prayed as well.

By now it was late morning. I was on my own, resting on the bed, when Wesley Adams, our local Methodist Minister, suddenly appeared. Sometimes we went to this church, as it was local. Wesley is a truly lovely born again pastor and, at that time, he and his wife Gloria had a Counselling Ministry.

"I have never seen you look so calm and so much at peace," said Wesley.

It was then that I realised calmness, stillness and peace really *had* come over me. I could not explain how or why, yet there it was deep in my heart. The Lord was moving and it was due to believers' prayers for me. The Lord gave what I needed for that particular occasion. I have never experienced it before or since.

"I have seen Matthew," explained Wesley, "I have been praying that he might be made whole."

"What do you mean by wholeness?" I inquired.

He went on to clarify. I felt then that the Lord was preparing me for what lay ahead, but I had not given up hope of a miracle. Wesley was a great help to me. I felt uplifted and encouraged by his visit. He really cared and understood.

I was still terribly tired and weak and needed to rest when I could. It was about 2.30 in the afternoon, when someone stirred me from my rest. "Come quickly." I knew straight away, something was seriously wrong with the baby. Matthew had had a bad time with his blood pressure and his pulse had gone haywire. The end looked very near. Paul had joined me and we phoned my father to break the news to him. To my amazement, he broke down in tears and I had the difficult task of comforting him.

"We must be prepared in our hearts for this," said Dad.

Somehow I held on to the Lord. His peace and stillness swept over me and gave me strength.

There was another Christian nurse on duty that afternoon, which seemed amazing. I believe now that God had planned it that way. After talking to her, we discovered that she was the sister of a friend of ours, who attended our local church. It was through God's goodness and grace that there seemed to be so many Christian nurses available, when we needed them most. I shared with the nurse that it was our wedding anniversary and how unfair it all was.

This was to be our last time with Matthew. His pulse and blood pressure worsened and there was no hope naturally speaking. Despite this, Paul and I took it in turns to massage Matthew's heart and keep it beating, prolonging the inevitable. Throughout this time we urged him to live, but I think he had had enough. A young doctor appeared and asked us if we were prepared to turn off the ventilator. What was he saying? Would we be prepared to kill our child? We were both shocked. Neither of us wanted the responsibility. Paul said he could not do it and suddenly it was all left to me.

The Lord helped me to make the choice, giving me the courage. Our baby breathed his last.

Chapter Six

The Aftermath

Nothing seemed real. The longed for baby was gone and all our expectations were dashed. There was nothing. I did not even cry, remaining calm, cool and collected. It was all over. The nightmare wasn't a nightmare -- it was an actual reality. By contrast, my husband found it all too much. He had been so brave during all the tension, but now it overflowed and he sobbed his heart out. The old idea, that men should never cry, is wrong. They have feelings and emotions, just like the so-called *fairer sex*. I am not implying I was braver. Perhaps, I was too numb to react at that point. I only know that the tears did not come.

When we next saw Matthew, his tubes had been removed and Paul took a photo. Finally, Matthew looked at peace. The nurses had laid him out and had even laid a yellow rose with him. We didn't even hold him after his death. Maybe, it would have helped the grieving process. Nevertheless, I remember saying to him: "You will always be loved. Any other children we have will know of you. You were our first child and you are very special. No one will take your place."

Paul's mother arrived, just before Matthew was due to be taken away. We knew her affectionately as 'Mutti' (a German variation of Mother). Paul had lived for a few years in Germany, learning the German language and culture. Mutti had a very strong personality, yet was kind, outgoing, bubbly and extrovert by nature, as well as being an intelligent woman. She had been a local councillor and belonged to social groups such as 'The Women's Institute' and 'Happy Circle' etc. Mutti kept herself busy until she was well into her seventies -- cleaning the local bank and helping to run the Plumney Flower Show. Unlike today, if you came from a poor background in Mutti's time, you were denied the chance to excel and reach your full potential. Her father had been a hard working farm labourer and foreman. For people like Paul's mother, university was just a pipe dream. Women were expected to marry and have children.

Despite being such a strong character, seeing Matthew dead proved too much for Mutti and she broke down completely. I didn't know it at the time, but she had lost a precious baby herself. She had never spoken about her experience to me.

I am ashamed to say that even if she had, I am not sure how I would have reacted. I remember our old neighbours, Mr and Mrs Richardson. I had often wondered why this lady and her husband never had any children. On investigation, my mother informed me that Mr and Mrs Richardson had lost not one, but two little girls to a stillborn tragedy. I had been saddened by this, and found it painful but deliberately suppressed it and pretended it wasn't real.

Mutti had always advised leaving buying certain things until after the baby was born, just in case something happened. I had never allowed myself to think very deeply about that (perhaps, it was a form of self-defence). Clearly, it all revived some old and very painful memories for her.

We said our farewell to Matthew. Much of this is vague for me. On returning to the post-natal ward, I found I had been moved to a side-room with another lady. She had her baby with her, which was rather insensitive of the hospital staff, I thought. It was all too much for me. I was jealous. I should have had a baby with me too, but our baby was dead. I don't think I cried even then, but my emotions were running high. The doctor came in, and asked if I wanted to go home, as there was no reason for me to remain. I jumped at the chance to get away from all those mothers with their babies. The doctor decided it would be a good idea if Paul and I took a sleeping tablet for the night. I reluctantly agreed. Pastor Bates arrived with Linda and they quickly weighed up the situation, immediately offering to drive us home. Paul was in no fit condition to drive. It did not take long to pack and I was soon ready to leave. I had arrived at the hospital three weeks ago with such high hopes. Would I ever know the joy of motherhood?

Paul's mother drove her own car to our house and she stayed with us for a few days. I know she meant well but, looking back, I wonder if we would rather have been on our own just then. I don't think I really took in her decision to stay in any case. Still, it was lovely to be at home, away from the hospital, even though I remained physically drained. Despite our deep sadness, we both managed to sleep fitfully as a result of the sedation we had been given. When we woke next morning, the memories of the previous day came flooding back to haunt us. I remained in bed. Mutti was determined that I was going to rest. She was afraid that I was going to over exert myself and cause damage that might mean I would not be able to conceive again. I felt frustrated. The telephone kept ringing and I wanted to answer it. I longed to talk about Matthew and let my feelings go.

Although I had lost the baby, the midwife still visited me. She was another Christian nurse that proved a comfort and an inspiration to me. I seem to remember her saying that she had a baby late in life and what joy the child had given her. She seemed to understand how I felt.

The long, hard labour had left me very sore. The midwife recommended a special cushion for me to sit on, available through the Red Cross. This proved to be a success and gave me some relief.

Friends visited and comforted us in our distress. Even Dr Emerson visited to give us the support we needed. He was clearly shaken by the events. As previously mentioned I had been under the consultant, Mr Harrison. Dr Emerson felt that if I had been under *him*, he might have been able to get the baby out quicker -- before any serious harm was done. He wished that he had had the opportunity to deliver the baby. He may have been able to spare us all the heartache. But it was too late. Nothing could bring Matthew back. The doctor said that if I had another baby, extra care would be given. I would receive VIP treatment and be monitored more carefully.

I did not mind talking about another baby already. In discussing this, I did not feel I was betraying Matthew. Could it happen again? Nothing could guarantee that history would not repeat itself. Obviously I would need a Caesarean next time, which was safer for the baby, but not quite as safe for me.

My memories of the days immediately after Matthew's death are vague and distant. I am amazed, as I look back, that Paul and I managed to sleep at night, yet we did. Perhaps it was God's grace.

I was tremendously aware that, behind the scenes, our Christian friends were praying for us and sharing the burden with us. We weren't alone. I believe the Lord literally carried us through the heartache and pain. Even the neighbours in our road came together to present us with a flowered ornament at our time of loss -- it was good to know people cared.

The Lord, I believe, used this heartache to bring Paul and me closer together. It had been a long time since we had felt that close. Perhaps we never had been, but we were now. It was about this time that my mother-in-law told me about Stephen. During the war, she had given birth to a son with Spina Bifida. He had lived for three weeks and then died. With her husband away at war, she was left to manage as best as she could alone.

"In those days," Mutti went on, "you were left to carry on regardless. You didn't have any counselling or discuss it with friends. Life just went on."

Then she added, almost as an afterthought, "It was far kinder. Today they do like to drag things on so."

Her remarks shocked me. They seemed cruel and I was hurt. How could that be the kindest thing for a bereaved person? How could she really believe what she had said? But she did.

"When I lost my husband," Mutti continued, "they expected me to stay working at the bank as if everything was fine. I thought it was cruel at the time. Now I realise it was the best thing that could have happened to me."

I firmly disagreed with her and said so. It soon became obvious we were not going to agree on the matter. What is right for one person isn't necessarily right for another!

Mutti had planned to stay with us until the funeral, but it was obvious our relationship was becoming more and more strained. On the Monday or Tuesday she left, leaving us alone. Matthew had been gone since the previous Friday.

Paul had felt totally unable to face work and had been signed off for three weeks, with nervous disorder. A dear lady from the church had rung Paul's factory and explained the position to them. They were kind and supportive, something I was not able to fully grasp at the time. I was just relieved that neither of us was left to face this ordeal on our own. We needed one another so very much.

It was during this first week that Brian, the manager of the local Christian bookshop, came to see us. He and his wife had lost a baby girl at birth, because the umbilical cord had strangled the child. How tragic for them! The child's name was Naomi.

"What a lovely name," I thought. "I wouldn't mind naming our child Naomi."

Brian went on to explain the feelings his wife and he had experienced following the death of their child. I have forgotten much that was said, but one thing I strongly recollect was a poem they gave us, which was very appropriate. Although Matthew hadn't been stillborn and the poem was entitled 'Stillborn', it could not have been more relevant to us. Unfortunately I am unable to quote from 'Stillborn' now, as part of this poem seems to be missing. Despite frantically searching the Internet for it, my attempts have been in vain, so reluctantly I have omitted the poem from this book. I have no publishing rights to include it in my story anyway.

I knew one thing -- people cared so very much. The letters and sympathy cards arrived daily. People seemed to know what to say, even though the majority were not Christians.

We were told we needed to grieve for a while. It was a healthy thing to do and part of the healing process.

"But no-one knows how it feels," I thought. "I don't know anyone who has lost a baby."

We felt so alone. Of course, as I reflect now, Mutti had also lost a well-loved child, but somehow that truth stayed hidden from me right then. It took time to make me realise we weren't unique. Other people had lost babies too.

My father had been due to attend a wedding in France, but on hearing of Matthew's illness and subsequent death, had remained in England. Dad came over on the Monday. He was a source of strength to me at the time. Dad and Paul had the task of registering Matthew's birth and then his death. Together they arranged Matthew's funeral for the following Friday.

We chose the Co-operative Funeral Directors as they had an excellent reputation in the area and their prices fell within what we could afford. Dad stayed with us for a while to discuss the last few days. He wondered if maybe Matthew had had something wrong with his lungs. Perhaps his lungs had functioned inside me, but couldn't work once he was born? I had not thought of that, and any explanation was welcome to me as it seemed to give me some peace of mind.

"I feel so numb, so empty," I said. "Will it ever pass?"

"Yes," assured my Dad. "Even in a month you will feel better."

I wondered how he could be so sure. But I had confidence in him. I felt he was right.

It was awkward to decide who would take the funeral service for us as we attended two churches. Yet this difficult problem was wonderfully overcome. Terry Bates, of the AoG, agreed to hold the service there. Wesley Adams, our Methodist Minister, was willing to help with the service and an old friend of ours, Reg Ashby, also a Pastor, was prepared to support us. Matthew could not be buried at the AoG, as there was no burial ground at this site. We knew there was a cemetery at the Methodist Church and Paul and I were very relieved and thankful when permission was granted for us to bury Matthew there. It was only two minutes' walk from our house, so the location was ideal.

I spent a lot of time thinking and I remember wondering if

maybe God had planned the tragedy for us to be able to show others His grace, in the midst of such difficult circumstances. I come from a nominal Christian background, perhaps this was the only way He could win those that Paul and I loved for Christ. I felt it would be worth the suffering if someone were to come to the Lord as a result of it. Somehow, such thoughts made the pain easier to bear.

There was a programme on television around this time that I believe was entitled '*The Lost Babies.*' Everyone had different stories to tell. One couple had given birth to a child whose brain had not developed normally. The child had been able to survive in the womb, but died soon afterwards. Although such instances are extremely rare, they are probably more common than people realise. Another older couple had unfortunately had a stillborn child.

A few days before the funeral, I was well enough to go with Paul to the florist to make arrangements as to what type of wreath we wanted. As we travelled into town, it felt to me like every second woman was either pregnant or pushing a newborn baby in a pram. I was jealous.

"What do they think of me?" I wondered. "I stand out. I haven't got a child. I'm different."

I failed to see that these people were too busy, too preoccupied with their own lives, to notice me. I was helplessly paranoid.

Paul and I had decided that we wanted something unusual for a wreath. We chose to have it formed into a cross, with an assortment of colours such as red, yellow and white. It was truly beautiful. Paul and I decided to ring up the Chapel of

Rest shortly before the funeral. This was to see if we could visit Matthew once more, before his burial. The attendant advised us not to look at his body, but to just remember him as he was. It was an awesome and lovely moment when Paul and I were left alone with Matthew. His body was in a very tiny white coffin. Of course it was not really he, just the shell of his body, as his spirit had departed at death.

We told Matthew again that we would always love him. We reminded him he was our first-born child and was very special. Once more, we told him no other child could take his place and we would make sure any child or children we had in future would know all about Matthew's short lifespan. Matthew had existed. He was a person and a unique individual in his own right. I recall saying to Matthew "You are loved, so wanted, and so very precious." We remained with his coffin for a while and then said goodbye for what would be the last time.

It was whilst we were at the Undertakers that we met a man who informed us that he and his wife had lost a baby. Tragically, they had not been able to have any more children. I felt sick at heart. I could not bear the thought of being childless, different to everybody else. It was my dream to bear children -- it was everything to me. I have already spoken of Catherine as being my favourite doll as a child. In my imagination, I had been a teacher and Catherine had been my special pupil. Sooty was her brother and I loved them dearly.

"One day when I grow up," I had thought, "I'll have a big family of my own. I really look forward to that day. It will be wonderful. I will have four children."

Naturally, I had forgotten that those children would also become adults.

We returned home. I felt saddened and flattened. I could not forget that man's plight. Paul and I had to decide what hymns we wanted for the funeral. Paul was from a Baptist background and was more familiar with the 'old' hymns than me. He chose '*There's a Friend for Little Children.*' I hadn't even heard of the hymn, but the more I read the lines, the more sure I was that this was right for Matthew. One particular verse stood out more than any other: '*No home on earth is like it, nor can with it compare, for everyone is happy, nor could be happier there.*' Together, we chose '*What a Friend we have in Jesus!*' We also had '*The King of Love my Shepherd is*' which Terry Bates selected.

The day of the funeral finally dawned. I was disappointed to see a dull miserable day. Was even the sun going to be denied us? The morning moved steadily on and I hung on to my hope that the weather would at least brighten slightly. It was not to be. We arrived at the funeral service about noon. It was a touching service. Terry Bates spoke on how King David had lost a son and had been heartbroken at the time. King David said, "*I will go to him, but he will not return to me,*" (*2 Samuel 12:23*). David and Bathsheba, his wife, then went on to have four other children. He concluded, "Maybe you too will know this joy." I must admit that I felt a bit sceptical then. Somehow I couldn't picture myself with four children. It was now beyond my wildest dreams.

Other people besides the family were there. My neighbour

Eva was present, as well as Paul's old friends from former days, Mr and Mrs Punt, and a friend of my father's called Mark.

I was very much aware of the Lord's presence throughout the service, but especially when the hymns were being sung. The Lord knew and He cared. Once the service was over, we made the short journey back to our local Methodist Church. Slowly, Matthew's little white coffin was lowered into the churchyard ground. It seemed as if all contact with him had gone forever. We were completely cut off and it was as if Matthew had never been. Suddenly holding the entire nightmare back, all the 'trying to cope' and 'putting on a brave face' took its toll. I didn't care anymore. My defences were down. It did not matter what other people thought. I cried out to the Lord, "Why, Lord Why?" and the tears welled.

We went out for a meal in a restaurant. It was just family and friends. Paul's mother was there of course, plus his brother Gerry, and his wife Rosemary who was expecting their second child. My brother had come too, but Frances, of course, was busy attending to young Michael. My mother had been unable to attend because she was unwell. Despite this, we somehow managed to have a pleasant time, even though it was a sober occasion.

Rosemary said the things I needed to hear. She reminded me I could have another baby; I was not in the sad position of being infertile. Matthew hadn't died a cot death and surely that would have been even worse, she concluded.

Rosemary told me of a couple she knew who had no hope of having children. How much worse for them! I shuddered in full agreement.

The meal ended and suddenly the family were all gone. Once more we were left to face the future alone.

Chapter Seven

Some kind of normality

Paul returned to work and I was left to struggle as best I could to regain some kind of normality. One thing I especially enjoyed every Tuesday was the mothers' get-together for prayer, Bible study, coffee and general chitchat. It was a time I could be free, yes, free to be myself and talk openly about what had happened. I didn't feel a nuisance. In fact, I was aware of the fact that people genuinely cared and would support me all the way. I met one lady there by the name of Moira. She said she felt sure that within three months, I would be pregnant again. I loved that thought, but dismissed it as being unduly optimistic. Such things don't happen to people like me! I prudently took her remarks as being her own good will rather than of the Lord. I hope that did not offend her feelings.

I so wanted it to be true, though! I wonder now why I pushed God out. Isn't He a good God who loves His children and wants good things for them? My picture of Him had become tainted. I saw God now as a somewhat distant figure that was out of touch with ordinary people. I felt He held a stick in one hand and He was set to pounce on me if I stepped just slightly out of line. Of course, our Heavenly Father isn't like that at all, but right then that's how I saw Him. We used to hold these meetings in different people's homes, including my own. It was during one of these sessions that someone read from a book by a well-known Christian author, Catherine Marshall, who was asking a question I was very familiar with: why does God allow such terrible things to happen? After much debate, she concludes that the Lord has two wills -- His ideal perfect will and His permissive will. Sometimes He allows what we humans would consider horrifically tragic things to happen. Such things can be used for His own purpose and glory. Yet how can we bring out the best in these situations? I think what spoke to me especially is that Catherine Marshall had lost her first and third grandchildren in tragic circumstances. Thankfully two other grandchildren had survived. I asked to borrow the book. *Something More* was a great inspiration to me at the time, as I am sure it would be to others going through trying circumstances.

Certain words spoken to me at this time, although well intended, were very painful -- 'It was for the best,' especially infuriated me. I would find Christians readily quoting *Romans 8:28* at me: "*And we know that in all things God works for the good of those who love Him who have been called according to His purpose*". Looking back now, the scripture that would have really helped is probably *Jeremiah 29:11-13* where it says, "*'For I know the plans I have for you,' declares the Lord, 'plans to prosper you and not to harm you, plans to give you hope and a future. Then you will call upon me and come and pray to me, and I will listen to you. You will seek me and find me when you seek me with all your heart.'*"

But, I was still going to other people, rather than to the Lord. One day, Alice, one of my friends, surprised me by telling me that, whilst she had prayed for Matthew, she had known 'it was going to be no good.'

"What do you mean?" I asked.

"I just knew," she returned. It was a remark I wished had remained unspoken. It was now about two months after Matthew's death. Alice suggested I try going back to work and Wendy, another friend, amicably agreed. I seethed inside. How could returning to work solve all my problems? I was angry and I told them both how I felt.

"How can you possibly understand? Going to work can't change things. It won't put right what's happened - as if Matthew had never existed!"

I still had my heart set on having a family. I was not the kind of woman who could put her all into a busy and fulfilling career. I quoted, "*Delight yourself in the Lord and He will give you the desires of your heart*" (*Psalm 37:4*).

"Yes," agreed my friends. "But that does not necessarily apply to your situation."

I didn't delve any further into what this Scripture meant to them, and they didn't enlighten me voluntarily either. I cannot help wondering now if I should have pursued the subject more vigorously. As I look at this Scripture today, I conclude that very few believers truly delight in the Lord and, unfortunately, many of us therefore take it out of context. If we delight in the Lord, we will abide in Him, and therefore be close to Him, then His will becomes our will. We are intermingled -- as one.

I remembered the words, uttered one day, of a Christian work colleague. Gordon said that within two years I would have two children. He felt that if I was unable to bear children I would become resentful towards the Lord. I saw this as a weakness on my part, but could clearly recognise what he was implying. Of course at the time, I thought he meant two *living* children. It never entered my mind that one child would no longer be with us.

It was through these Tuesday meetings that I made further friends. I was introduced to two new Christians, Nicola Green and Freda Parker. Alice and her husband, David, had been used by the Lord to help these dear ones find the Lord Jesus Christ. I vaguely knew Nicola from one previous meeting. She had invited me to go to a local seaside town with her and her three children. We had a lovely time there. I can't fully understand it, but I believe it was by God's grace that Nicola and I just clicked. She was to become one of my best Christian friends from that day forward. Nicola is a busy housewife and mother with many special qualities, one of which, to me in particular, is that she is a good listener. No matter her hectic schedule, she always has time to listen. Nicola is a natural person, with no airs or graces, and she accepted me as I was. That acceptance was something I was in great need of after all my early struggles to be someone I was not and to 'fit in'. Truly the Lord's timing is perfect and I can only thank God for His care and concern for me, through Nicola.

Every Friday seemed to bring back memories of Matthew. I think this was because Matthew died on a Friday and I unwittingly associated that day of the week with his death. I am glad to say that, in time, this gradually faded away naturally.

We were also indebted to the Rev. Wesley Adams and his wife Gloria, who were mightily used by the Lord to help us come to terms with what had happened. One day, prior to the funeral, Wesley had spoken about how I had been deprived of being a mother. I had not even thought of it like that. He seemed to be reassuring me that I had a right to grieve, given that what I was expecting had been taken from me. Wesley continued, wondering if, one day, I would have a daughter and she would be a missionary. He was already thinking ahead.

"A missionary? That would be good," I thought. Was he saying something prophetic? We were to see Wesley and Gloria several times over the next few months. There was one occasion when Wesley asked if we were prepared to forgive God for Matthew's death. I couldn't understand what he meant. God doesn't sin. It seemed wrong to me to forgive One who cannot sin. Quietly, and calmly, Wesley explained: I was quite right in my belief that God could not sin; yet I had become angry, bitter and resentful toward Him. He was right! God is an all-powerful, all-knowing, all-loving God and yet He had allowed Matthew's death. What had I done to deserve this? I had tried to live a godly life, endeavouring to please the Lord in every way. I was not like some people who seemed to live such carefree, immoral lives, doing whatever they pleased, without any fear of God, and seemingly getting away with it without suffering tragedies like mine. Yes, I *was* angry. I just didn't understand! I had forgotten completely what the Bible has to say about such people: "*But the wicked will perish. The Lord's enemies will be like the beauty of the fields, they will vanish - vanish like smoke*" (*Psalm 37:20*). There are other references to the ungodly throughout God's Word.

We realised that we had to admit our angry feelings and ask God to forgive us. Then we had to forgive God for allowing such a horrific event to happen to us. We were not healed overnight, but gradually and gently, it seemed, the Lord was remoulding us so that we could accept Matthew's death and get on with life.

I can't say it was all plain sailing though. There were setbacks too. Paul and I had a holiday in November, just two months after Matthew's death. We returned to a Christian centre in Devon where we had been only months before, when I was expecting Matthew. In a conversation with the husband of the family we were staying with, I recalled my almost obsessive desire to become pregnant and mused that perhaps I had wanted a child too much. He agreed that I might be right. I was devastated. I had expected and wanted him to say he was sure that wasn't the case! When he agreed with me, I had great difficulty accepting what I'd heard. Was he saying God was punishing me somehow? It was to be some time before I could put these thoughts out of my mind. With the benefit of hindsight, I can bring to mind other Christian believers who are equally desperate for a baby. God is no more punishing them than he punished me! God is a good God. If this were the case, what about Hannah who fervently prayed for a child and was rewarded by having the prophet Samuel? This story is beautifully recorded in the first chapter of Samuel.

Overall, I found older people more hardened, less sympathetic, to our story. We visited two of Paul's friends who were now in an old people's home. Paul had met this couple many years before, when he had travelled with them and others in a group to Israel. The wife did most of the talking. Yes, she had known a young couple that had lost their first child soon after birth. The woman concerned went on to have a miscarriage. It had seemed that success had come the third time but unfortunately, after three days, the baby, who was already ill, grew worse and then died. This was hardly the thing I wanted to hear so soon, just two months after our sadness. How heart breaking! These people were also Christians. The only encouraging thing that came out of this heartache was that eventually the couple were able to adopt and have children that way.

Yet for me the hurt had been planted. It was a while before I realised I had to forgive this woman for telling me something that I would rather not have known about. As I look back I can only marvel at the Lord, for He helped me to ride each individual storm as it happened and I do recall coming home from our holiday refreshed and renewed.

Soon afterwards, Paul and I visited his Grandmother in hospital. Known to us all as Nana, she had worked very hard in a shop in the village where she lived and was well known to the locals. Poor Nana had lost her leg to gangrene, but she kept reasonably bright and cheerful. It was to be the last time we saw her. One of the last things she said to us was, 'You may never have a baby again.' Yet somehow this time, though I experienced hurt, I in no way felt the same deep anguish I had previously suffered.

Shortly before Christmas that year, Helen Robinson's niece, my old nursing colleague and friend, invited me over to visit her in her new flat. She had lived for many years in the Nurses Home and now finally had a place of her own. Wanda Smith had never been that close to me, but we had got on amicably together. In words that I was now very familiar with, she too suggested that it was possible I may never have another baby. 'Here it comes again', I said to myself as the conversation began. But, somehow the Lord was teaching me and strengthening me through this. I seemed able to take it now and, even though I didn't like it, accept that Wanda could well be right.

Even so, shortly after Matthew's death, I had stood up in church and quoted a Scripture that the Lord had shown me. Some time before falling pregnant, I had earnestly sought from Him if it were His will for me to have children or not. His answer had come from *Psalm 113 v 9*: "*He settles the barren woman in her home as a happy mother of children.*" The Lord had given me this Scripture not once, but twice. Now, in church, I just *had* to question His apparent promise. He had said this scripture was for me at that particular time. He had given me this when I was honest and open with Him.

I didn't understand what had happened! Paul and I were visiting a church we hardly knew, but I had to be obedient and express, even in the presence of relative strangers, what I felt the Lord had placed on my heart and say it anyway.

I knew Matthew was now in heaven. Our friend, Roy Clarkson, told me on one occasion that Matthew was totally unlike the rest of us: whilst we have all become marred by sin, Matthew had never sinned. Yes, he had inherited sin, but he had been shielded because he died so soon after birth. Matthew's relationship with His Heavenly Father was different. It was truly very special.

Yes, I know I probably come across as being completely split. Part of me believed I could go on to have another child, but another big part was extremely wary and cautious. Maybe I had misunderstood the Scripture and the verse wasn't from the Lord after all? Yes, there were doubts there alright.

One day we went over to see my parents. Mum and Dad had invited us. Frances and Paul and their newborn baby, Michael, were within easy walking distance, but it was no good. We did not feel up to seeing our nephew. The memories of the past few months, the feeling that there should have been two babies, not one, still hit us vividly. One day we would have to face it, and the time couldn't be delayed forever, but we weren't ready yet.

We had a visitor whilst we were at the farm. Mum and Dad had invited their vicar, the Rev Stanley Brown, to talk to us. He and his wife had also lost their first child, but they had gone on to have two more children. They seemed to be of the opinion that losing one's first child was quite common. I was to learn that Neo-natal death, and stillbirths, are a far more frequent occurrence than the much feared and dreaded cot death.

I haven't yet spoken about how Paul was taking Matthew's death. In some ways, he seemed to be taking it worse than me. He hadn't been as close to the Lord as he ideally should have been and now, it seemed to him, God was avenging this and punishing him for his lack of commitment. Paul had said soon after Matthew's death, and many times later, 'Poor Matthew.' Some people took this to mean, 'Poor Paul' as well. In some ways they were quite right, but then, they had never experienced such trauma first hand. I, myself, found it difficult to comprehend how a man could be so saddened by the death of his newborn baby. Unlike me, Paul had not carried Matthew for nine months, which had of course entailed feeling Matthew's movements and getting attached to the lump inside me. Perhaps the most natural and simple thing to have done at such a time was simply to accept that I didn't understand, to accept that Paul needed help and support just as much as I did. Perhaps more than myself! I can't help wondering, as I look back, if I could have done more to see Paul through this difficult period, instead of being as concerned as to how *I* was coping.

In these early days just after Matthew's death, when it was still very raw, some of our Christian friends and I became very concerned about Paul. He kept going to Matthew's grave and persisted in praying that Matthew would come back to life. Sheila, a dear friend, eventually helped by suggesting to us that it would be unkind to expect Matthew to return to earth, after knowing the joys of Heaven.

The time came for my postnatal check-up. Paul and I went together. Yes, physically I was fine. Everything had gone back into place. I should certainly be able to conceive again. After three normal periods, I could try to conceive again. Knowing what they had been like in the past, I prayed to myself that they *would* start! The Consultant, Mr Harrison, then went on to explain why Matthew had died. He made no excuses and no cover up. Matthew need not have died. It was human error -- if the doctor had acted quickly enough Matthew would probably be alive today. He had died as a result of cerebral anoxia (lack of oxygen to the brain). The doctor, on arriving on the ward, should have straight away used forceps, instead of waiting as he did. If he had, then the outcome could have been very different. The baby had been quite normal, according to the post-mortem. The doctor who had delivered Matthew had moved away to another hospital in London.

"How convenient!" I thought rather harshly.

Yet, I was thankful at least that there had been no attempt to conceal the truth from us. It was out in the open. We could even sue if we so desired. Now, there were other voices coming from everywhere. Diane told me of a friend of hers who had lost a baby boy in similar circumstances. She had taken the hospital to court. Then Polly, a flamboyant character in our Tuesday group, suggested the same thing.

I couldn't believe what I was hearing. I was a Christian, a follower of Jesus Christ. Didn't Jesus show mercy, love and compassion? It hardly seemed very forgiving to go ahead with a court case. I pointed this out to Polly.

"Yes, but others may suffer in the future if you don't take action." she returned.

I was not convinced, but one thing I definitely did wrong -- I didn't pray. I just chose to abandon the idea. Paul, though, made the decision for us. We would not sue. After all, no amount of money would bring Matthew back. I must admit, I do wonder now if we did the right thing. We might not have won the case, but if we had, the money may have come in handy. All such motives are probably wrong and, for that reason, we almost certainly did the *right* thing.

Christmas was approaching and, not long afterwards, a New Year. I could not wait to see the back of 1983. The year had begun so promisingly and had ended for us so tragically. Yet there was another shock in store for the family. Paul's Nana had been ill with pneumonia and, on Christmas Eve, she died. 'What a year,' I thought bitterly.

It was a sad, unhappy Christmas that year. Mutti did her best to put on a brave face. As she said, Nana, after all, was spending Christmas in heaven, which was far better than any earthly experience.

"We needn't be sad," she said to Paul, who had enjoyed a close relationship with Nana. "I wonder if Matthew and Nana have met yet. I expect so."

A little later it was time for Nana's funeral. Paul had been off work with a stomach bug and was not in a fit condition to drive too much, so his brother kindly helped us out. Nana's hymns were bright and cheerful. She had chosen, '*And can it be?* and '*We're marching to Zion.*' There were two services, one at the local church by a Baptist Minister, and the second at Oxbury Crematorium. Nana's suffering was over. But why had she had to endure so much hardship? Couldn't she have died under the anaesthetic while she was having her her leg amputated? Her final years of sickness just seemed so pointless. There they are again, Lord. These nagging questions that always seem to be there.

I spoke quite freely about Matthew at the reception and I was shocked sometime later when Mutti said to me, 'I'm not going to tell you who, but someone said at Nana's funeral that you were making too much fuss about your experience. They thought you should have been over it by now.' I felt almost dumbstruck. Who had it been? This new hurt struck deep inside me. Could it have been a member of the family? I wanted to know and somehow make this person pay for being so callous (as they seemed to me then). Or perhaps they were right and I didn't want to admit it? I think it was harder for people to understand our grief, because they could not equate Matthew's death with that of a person who had lived a life. Stillbirth or a neonatal death is just as heart breaking to the loved ones left behind. It is only others who regard it as different, something 'lesser than.'

It is so complex for us bereaved parents. We are grieving for a baby we never knew. What would Matthew have been like if he had lived? What would he have looked like? We had been deprived of having a relationship with him on earth. I will not be his mother in heaven, but will have an even better relationship there with him than I could possibly have here below. This did not seem possible then and, even today, I cannot begin to imagine or visualise the reunion.

1984 arrived and another year started. This served to heighten my awareness that I should have had a baby with me at the beginning of this New Year and, inwardly, I fumed in frustration. After all, Mutti had another child within a year of her loss. It was around this time that Rosemary, my pregnant sister-in-law, had to be admitted to hospital. She was losing water and she was confined to bed rest. Poor thing -- she would be staying in hospital even longer than I had done. How unfortunate! We didn't know then, but life was not going to be kind to her and Gerry. Rosemary was constantly in my thoughts and prayers as I prayed to the Lord to keep the baby safe and not to let the same thing happen to her. Unfortunately, we weren't able to visit her because she lived some way from us.

Wesley and Gloria had kindly contacted a Christian they knew, who had lost her baby. Would I like to go along to her neonatal and stillbirth group? I hesitated at first. I did not need that. I could cope. Later, however, I decided I had nothing to lose. Sandy lived about two miles away in Ambone. Her first baby, a boy, had been born prematurely and hadn't had the strength to survive. She had heard him utter a cry, but a few minutes later he was dead. Nowadays, Sandy explained, her child would probably have survived as hospital facilities have advanced and improved so much since this sad episode.

Sandy drove me to the meeting. I did not know what to expect and it was not quite as I had imagined. No one seemed to be talking about his or her dead babies. It could have been any women's get together, I thought, somewhat unbelievingly. I was determined to break the ice. What were their experiences? What had happened to them? Yes, bit-by-bit I coaxed it out of them. After all, I had not come to this gathering to sit around gossiping. I needed to know the facts. Emily, the lady of the house we were visiting, struck me especially. She had the agonising heartache of two tragedies, close together. She had lost a baby girl at nine months from cot death and then went on to lose a baby boy at birth. Emily had five other children, all boys.

"Surely," I said, "cot death is worse." Her answer surprised me.

"Well, I don't know. At least I had time to get to know my daughter. With my son, there was nothing."

Emily was someone who had experienced both cot death and neonatal death first hand, and it was obvious to me what she thought was worse.

I was feeling more able to cope now. It was late February 1984, five months after Matthew's death, when I was to have another brush with tragedy.

The phone rang on that fateful Monday morning. Marty, a Christian in the village, had been speaking to her mother on the phone, when she complained of feeling unwell and dizzy. Her mother quickly dialled the phone number of Marty's neighbours -- Alice, who I have mentioned earlier, and her husband David. They were absolutely shocked at what they found when they went round. Marty, at the age of thirty-one, had suffered a severe heart attack (not known at the time), and was fighting for her life. She had a rare heart condition that had not been detected. I believe her children have since had to be tested to ensure they are not at risk of this condition as well. The ambulance was called, but there was little they could do. Marty was dead. I was upset that day, but on the next day, a wellmeaning Christian further aggravated my feelings.

It was the Tuesday meeting again and we were all discussing the terrible events of the previous day. Marty had left behind a husband and two young children aged seven and four. How was he going to cope? Would Robert re-marry? What would this do to his relationship with the Lord?

I remember sharing that it all brought back memories of when I lost Matthew. Polly, who I have mentioned previously, stated in a matter of fact manner that I should have been over that by now. It was more than I could take. The hurt boiled within me and I burst into tears. Nicola and some friends comforted me and, after a good cry, I felt better. A little while later, Polly contacted me. She came around to my house and our relationship was restored. Praise the Lord for that! Robert did eventually meet someone else. He remarried and had another child, so the Lord blessed him in his heartache.

Ten days later, Rosemary gave birth to her second child. Gerry rang to say they had a baby boy, but he didn't seem as excited as parents do on the birth of a new child. Something seemed to be wrong. It wasn't long before we knew why. Christopher had Down's syndrome. 'Not another catastrophe!' I thought bitterly. First it was Paul and me, now Rosemary and Gerry. Frances agreed it was sad for the family as a whole, but pointed out that Rosemary and Gerry were the ones who would ultimately carry the burden.

"That's why she nearly miscarried," said Mutti.

It seemed so callous and heart breaking. Rosemary had spent so much time resting in hospital, only to have a Down's syndrome child at the end. It wasn't fair! Why does this sort of thing happen? What have we done to deserve it? Rosemary had undergone having a stitch in her cervix, to ensure the baby's safety, and now this. No one had offered a test to see if the baby had this condition -- Rosemary was only thirty and it was thought she was too young for her baby to be at risk. Mutti's last child had been born in her early forties. Helen was perfectly normal, yet Rosemary at thirty was having a Down's syndrome child. It just didn't seem right.

It was about this time, in March 1984, when we were able to give Matthew his headstone in the local Methodist churchyard. We had chosen a marble tombstone representing the Bible, depicting words from *Luke 24 v 5b & 6a. King James Version*. The words written on the tombstone, in the shape of a book, read, '*Why seek ye the living among the dead for he is not here. He has gone to be with Jesus. For many dear children are gathered there for such is the kingdom of heaven* † *Safe in the arms of Jesus. Matthew Paul Turpin. Called home 30th Sept 1983 aged 1½ days, so precious, so loved.*'

It was time to see the gynaecologist again. He gave us the necessary 'go ahead' to start the fertility drug again. It was discovered that I needed a higher dose to ovulate this time. I found this discouraging, but if the outcome were a pregnancy and a baby at the end, what would it matter?

May of 1984 was an exciting time for us Christians. Billy Graham was coming to Britain and was visiting a town not far from us! At that time, I was in a Prayer Triplet Group. We were praying for three different people each, so altogether nine people received prayer. I think, as I look back, that May was the time I was finally over Matthew's death. I was excitedly looking to Billy Graham's Crusade with a real sense of expectancy. Wendy was to be a Counsellor. 'What about me?' I wondered. I really didn't have the confidence and it was too big a challenge. Surely I'd make a mess of it and fall flat on my face. I knew I ought to try harder, but that was as far as it went. I did not want the commitment, the time consumption etc. I suppose what I really wanted was an acceptable excuse, to justify my weakness!

In addition to Billy Graham's promised visit, Fiona Castle, the wife of well-known entertainer Roy Castle, came and spoke at the Baptist Church in town. She too had been an actress. She shared how Roy had been away a lot and times had often been very difficult, but giving her heart to the Lord had certainly helped her become more the person God had called her to be, and kept her in fresh hope.

Early June came and, with it, a much welcomed break from the usual routine in the form of a holiday. As previously mentioned, Paul had worked in Germany and had made many friends. He had felt accepted and found the people sociable and friendly. We stayed with Inge and Wolfgang Schipper. They attended the Pentecostal Church in Glücksburg, where they lived in a modern detached house. The house was spacious, with three storeys, including a cellar -- a common feature in Germany. Inge and Wolfgang were extremely hospitable hosts. Inge's mother of seventy-seven lived with them and they had two children, one-aged sixteen and the other six. The wide gap between the two children had hardly been Inge's choice. She had been pregnant three times, only for them all to end in miscarriage. Inge and Wolfgang had continued to persevere and in the end were rewarded with Jan. I found such stories uplifting and encouraging -- their persistence truly paid off. I reminded myself that my time would come. Jan was a lovely little boy and well worth waiting for. I could see that.

These were happy days and I was enjoying myself. There were no barriers, despite the language problem. My German is extremely limited and Inge's English was only slightly better. Paul acted as the go-between, so we were able to communicate reasonably well. Sometimes Wolfgang also helped, as he had a reasonable grasp of English.

One morning I woke up feeling rather faint. I don't know why, but I had a strange feeling I was pregnant. Whilst my period was over two weeks late, this was not uncommon for me. I had been taking my temperature and had thought that I hadn't ovulated, so how could I be expecting?

We returned to England and shortly afterwards my suspicions were confirmed. I was pregnant again, with our second child.

Chapter Eight

Pregnant again

I felt ecstatic and joyful to be pregnant once more! It didn't seem possible. The new baby was expected to arrive in February. Friends assured me that it would be a wonderful time to have a baby. He or she would be born just prior to spring, leaving me the long summer days to enjoy the child. Matthew had arrived on September 29th, making him almost a winter baby. I was happy and yet I was apprehensive too. Would anything go wrong?

It seemed to me that everyone I knew was pregnant. Frances was already expecting her second child after having Michael. Celia, my friend from nursing days, was expecting her first baby in October, and Nicola was expecting her fourth child in July. Now I was happily joining the clan and truly thankful to be part of it. No, I did not have any feelings of betrayal about Matthew. This was a new baby and the start of a new adventure. I think most people I knew shared my enthusiasm.

I had a scan that revealed the baby was doing fine, which I found thoroughly reassuring.

Paul and I had been finding our time at the Assembly of God Church a strain. With hindsight, though, I believe that we did make a bad mistake in deciding to leave the church then and go elsewhere to worship the Lord Jesus Christ. We were hardly young ourselves, yet most people seemed much older than us and I hungered to mix with younger people. We made this our excuse, or reason, for leaving the church. It seemed right at the time. No one was happy to see us go, however. I suppose the fellowship may have been hurt. They had looked after us and supported us so well in our time of need. Perhaps it seemed to them we were shutting them out, disregarding and ungrateful for all they had done for us.

I must admit, though, that both of us felt at home the moment we entered the Elim Church in Twinmere. There seemed to be an electric, joyful atmosphere there. One of the first things we noticed was how the Pastor, Reverend S. Licence, was so gentle and caring. For example, we witnessed him taking aside a young woman after she had prophesied. He had felt that this was not of the Lord and spoke to her in love. Everyone seemed so friendly and loving. We were certainly made to feel welcome and were soon put at ease. I especially bonded with the Pastor's wife, Joy. She had a quiet and gentle character and displayed much love. Yet the Lord had allowed her to be plagued with illness and, in the brief time I knew her, she was never well. Yet, it seemed to me that she truly lived out the Word. It is recorded in Scripture that, "*The joy of the Lord is your strength*" (*Nehemiah 8:10, King James Version*). Joy had cancer and needed a miracle. Here was a woman, firm in her faith, but who had suffered much. I was to learn later that Joy had lost a child at birth. Her husband told me this, and that they had five children between them. Surprisingly, Samuel and Joy had come to know the Lord on the same day, although in different places. I guess you could say that the Lord never makes a mistake.

Late June came and Paul and I arranged to go with our new church to hear Billy Graham give his talk. I was quite excited. I had never heard him speak before and now I was going to see the great man in person. I think what I failed to see is that it is never the person, but God, who we should be worshipping and exalting -- not the man merely talking about God.

I do not remember the sermon, but at the end I found myself up at the front, having felt the call to rededicate my life to the Lord. I spoke to a young counsellor about my son Matthew and my subsequent bereavement. Names and addresses were exchanged. I spoke to her about how I was now expecting again.

The day was hot and sticky. Suddenly, seemingly out of nowhere, I developed a thumping headache. I felt poorly and longed to be at home. I knew by the way I was feeling that a migraine attack was on its way. Frances and her father, who is also a Christian, were at the meeting. Somehow I managed to speak to them, but it wasn't easy with the pounding pain, right in my forehead. They were travelling on another coach and were about to go home. It seemed to take an age for our own coach to travel back to Twinmere. We had nearly made it home when the inevitable happened. I was violently sick, but very relieved to be almost home. It would be straight to bed without any supper for me!

My birthday was rapidly approaching. This year Paul was thinking of giving me something different, perhaps a little unusual, as a birthday gift – a little kitten. Paul had seen it advertised locally. We went round to the lady's house and it was all comparatively easy. We did not even have to choose. There was only one kitten left, a female, we were informed. This kitten was a ginger tabby with green eyes. She had a pretty face with a lovely smile. We took her home and called her Julie. It was much later, when we took her to the vet that we found out her true identity. Julie was male! What to call him now? "What about Julius?" suggested the vet "Perfect!" we answered, and we changed his name to Julius.

Our next-door neighbours, Eva and Luke, had also taken a kitten from the same litter. We fondly believed the two cats, brothers, would be the best of friends but this never materialised. Julius was domineering and extrovert in personality, whilst Sandy was nervous and introvert. I think having Julius helped us. In particular, it gave me something else to focus on.

I was relieved to get over the first trimester hump and told myself positively that things should be alright now. Nothing seemed to point to the contrary. Our doctor advised Paul to have a chromosomal blood test, because Christopher, the Down's syndrome child, was on his family's side. I prayed for it to be okay. My prayers were answered and I breathed again.

The Spina Bifida test also came back normal. Everything seemed to be going fine.

I carried on as before, doing a little painting in the house whenever I could. Yet I was slightly concerned -- this was my second baby and I hadn't felt a kick yet. Usually, one can be aware of the baby moving much earlier the second time around. I tried to reassure myself that it would come. Nothing was going to go wrong this time!

One day I was emptying Julius' litter tray as usual, when I slipped and fell heavily on my back. I was taken aback and shocked. Would the baby be alright? Of course it would, I decided. The baby was well protected in my womb and would be fine. I kept the accident to myself and didn't inform the doctor. It's easy to be wise after an event, though, and with hindsight I think I should have let him know. Anyway, I said nothing and carried on as before. I did not rest or change my lifestyle. A day or so later I thought I felt a kick. It was not strong and I was not convinced. It was to be the only time I was to experience this feeling during the pregnancy. Now, as I look back, I'm glad and thankful this happened, even if it was my imagination.

A former acting Pastor and his wife visited us. It was great to see Reg and Audrey Ashby. Despite the fact that they were of retiring age, they had felt the Lord's call to go to France and were just back in England, visiting family and friends. Audrey had not been a really healthy person for years, but always did her best to remain cheerful and positive. It was hard for her to live in a foreign country, as her French was somewhat limited, but if that was what the Lord wanted, who was she to stand in the way? Although a strong woman in her own right, as a wife I saw Audrey as truly submissive to her husband, as we should be according to Scripture. She certainly was no doormat, however!

Wednesday morning came. There was something wrong. I was beginning to bleed. I tried to stay calm, but it was not easy.

"O Lord, why?" I cried, "Please. Not again!"

Late afternoon came and the bleeding was getting worse. I now had severe abdominal pain, so Paul drove me to the doctor. I was immediately admitted to hospital - there was no hesitation. Paul took me there in the car. I was extremely nervous. I had a threatened miscarriage and instant action was necessary. On the way, we called in home and I gathered together some nightclothes and quickly filled a sponge bag. I could hardly believe what was happening and arrived on the Gynaecological Ward in a daze. I was placed on bed rest, but still had some distance to walk to the toilet. This distance troubled me, but there seemed nothing I could do about it. No, they could not move me. Somehow I managed to sleep that night and woke up next morning to more pain. There was no sign the pain was abating and I continued to bleed heavily. Yes, I would be given a scan in the afternoon, to see how the baby was doing. I found this reassuring and I looked forward to seeing the baby on the screen. Then the news came that the Radiographer was very busy and they couldn't fit me in that day. I felt numb. Why, why couldn't I have this small reassurance my heart yearned for?

Another patient told me that she, or it could have been

her friend, had bled heavily in one particular pregnancy and yet her baby was eventually born safely. I was slightly encouraged, but my heart cried out in fear as I prayed to God.

In spite of the encouraging story, I was becoming increasingly apprehensive. The pain had not eased and I was convinced something was very wrong. A young woman that I had befriended at the Tuesday evening prayer group came in to visit me that Thursday afternoon. She brought with her a book by James Herriot and I thanked her. At least I had something to read now. I barely knew her, but she was caring and practical and expressed genuine concern for me.

I couldn't understand why the gynaecologist was being so calm. Couldn't he see I was likely to miscarry? Couldn't he do something for me? Yes, my consultant had prescribed me painkillers, but other than that, he had done nothing, or so it seemed. He was really matter of fact, so annoyingly optimistic. Perhaps his manner should have been a source of comfort and strength to me, an inspiration, but somehow I did not fit into his mould. I think if the pain had been less intense, maybe I would have believed him. Yet, in all the discomfort, it was as if I already knew...I believe now that, once again, God was preparing me for what lay ahead.

Somehow, I managed to sleep for part of that night. I was awakened about three hours later, in the night, by a very sharp, intense pain. It was in the abdomen, a period like pain, but this time even worse than before.

"It could be bad wind," said the nurse. "Sometimes that can be really painful."

"Don't be so daft," I thought inwardly. "I know the difference between wind and severe period-like pain."

I needed the bedpan and asked for it. I knew almost for sure what had happened. I passed heavy clots of blood. The nurse took it away and it was not long before she returned.

"I've lost the baby haven't I?"

"Yes," came the reply, "I'm afraid so."

I wish, now, that I had asked to see the foetus, even if all I saw would have been blood. Our baby was dead, just like our first baby. It had happened again and with it came the agonising cry.

"Why? What was the Lord doing to us?"

Despite it all, I managed to sleep the remainder of the night. When Paul arrived to see me, he was almost as upset as me.

"We will try again, he assured me. "We won't give up."

These were the words I needed to hear, and they gave me a real boost.

Two Pastors also came to see me. The first to arrive was the Minister that had taken over from Wesley at the Methodist Church. Nathan was comparatively young and had a very lively personality. He was certainly good with children and knew how to bring them out. His sermons were always interesting and he had a unique gift of expressing himself so people were never bored. They liked his jokes and he was very popular. I did not know him well and was surprised by his visit. I questioned him as to whether I would have another child. He was tender, but also to the point. If something went wrong next time, he doubted if it was God's will for me to bear children. It was a question of wait and see.

Then Samuel also arrived. I explained to him I was worried about my age. I was thirty-one.

"You're still fairly young," he said. "Why, I've known people in their forties having babies. Don't give up."

I thanked him and felt better.

I saw Mr Harrison, who seemed genuinely surprised that I had miscarried. He was of the opinion that, despite my bleeding, everything should have proceeded normally. My losing the baby had certainly jolted him.

I was to have a womb scrape that afternoon. I was a bit nervous and was grateful for the prayers of Nathan and Samuel. I was led outside into the operating theatre, which, to my mind, was a bit primitive for this day and age. The theatre should have been under the same roof as the wards.

The surgery was soon over and I was amazed at how physically good I felt. Paul took me home the next day and I was informed that it would be two weeks before I was back to normal. The amazing thing was that this miscarriage was almost a year to the day since we lost Matthew.

I was very surprised at how quickly my body recovered. I began to nervously think about the future. Before this pregnancy, I had stayed at home, confident it would not be long before I would conceive again. It had happened, but to no avail. Was I going to stay at home, forever mothering myself, or should I now face the stark reality of work? The idea of going back to full time nursing did not appeal. I had no desire to take up that responsibility as yet. I just wanted something that would bring the pennies in and get me out of the house. What work could I do, I wondered? Part-time in the morning would be fine. I looked at the jobs in the Job Centre and there was one I felt drawn to. The job advertised was for a Part-Time Domestic, which would involve working in a Hospital for the Mentally Handicapped, as it was known then. Today, people previously referred to as 'Mentally Handicapped' are said to have 'Learning Difficulties' or a form of 'Special Needs', which to me is a far more kind and sensitive way of expressing such a disability.

I can't remember much about the interview, but it was very informal. I wondered out loud, given my references would have to be taken up, when I would know if I had the job or not? The answer surprised me totally.

"I'm offering you the job now," came back the reply. "Would you like it?"

"Well, yes please," I replied and then wondered how I would even get to work! We had sold the moped that had been so handy when I had worked full time at the local psychiatric hospital. It would have to be the bus. On my first day, I caught the No. 5 bus to the station and then changed to a No. 11 bus, which ran past the hospital. Self-consciously, I went to the Domestic Office to fetch the keys I would need for my work. All the other cleaners were doing the same thing. If I were late, they would know it.

I was shown to the villa in which I was to work. I liked the middle aged dark-haired woman who was to be my working colleague. My heart sank, though, when I realised what was expected of me in the time span. I was not the quickest of workers and I feared there would be times when I would experience great difficulty in coping. This could be a problem when Brenda my colleague had her day off. I could not begin to comprehend how I would survive, but now that I was in a job, I wanted to stay. The twenty-seven pounds per week my work brought in wasn't much, but at least it was better than no earnings at all.

I look back at this time with some regrets. Yes, I spoke to the nursing staff now and then, but I had an opportunity to learn how to relate to mentally handicapped adults and I blew it. I don't think it was pride or intentional unfriendliness. It was just that I was always busy and, to be honest, I don't even think I realised I was behaving this way at the time. I needed someone to approach me and tell me I was rather aloof with the patients, but no one actually did. Perhaps, the Lord was trying to prepare me for the future and I didn't know it. I had a job, which occupied my time and brought in money. That was all.

Senior nursing staff felt I was wasting my time as a domestic and should apply to work there as a nurse instead. Maybe one day, I thought, when I considered the matter. After all, I'm not mentally handicapped-trained; do I really want to spend more hours studying, delving into textbooks, writing essays, etc.? No, I was firmly convinced, definitely not. I would just come into mentally handicapped nursing as an outsider, even with the experience of being both a trained Nurse and also, more recently, a Psychiatric Nurse. Further training did not seem to be the right direction for me. My parents, especially my mother, weren't very encouraging about the prospect of my undergoing further nursing training, in this additional speciality. Perhaps it was ignorance or fear. I don't know, but their attitude did help to influence me in a negative way. And, anyway, I'd be pregnant again soon, wouldn't I? That was what was dearest to my heart after all.

I soon found I was not always to be working with Brenda. Every now and again we were moved, so I often had to work on my own without her. I rarely found time to have a break. It seemed a constant rush to wash and dry up, do the vacuuming and clean the bathrooms, sinks and toilets. I was often late off duty, because I had not managed to fit everything into the appropriate time. I was well known by management for working over my appointed hours.

"One thing about Jane," my Superior commented, "she might be slow, but she is thorough."

Now I was at work, I was meeting people from all walks of life. I was even working with young boys. They tended to keep themselves to themselves, but were generally work conscious as well as friendly. There was even one young girl of seventeen, with whom I was able to share my faith. I told her how I believed there was a reason for my suffering. She listened patiently, seeming to absorb what I was saying with genuine concern.

Yet, life wasn't always sweet. I am a sensitive person by nature and certain events brought back memories to me of when I had been bullied as a schoolgirl. It was happening again. There were two women at work with whom I didn't click and I began to dread working with them. They both worked on the children's ward.

Despite this, when I saw the young children on the ward, I

felt moved and touched. 'Why, Lord?' came the old question again. Many of the children were physically handicapped, on top of their mental condition. Their lives seemed pointless, mundane and without any meaning, purpose or direction.

"Why?" I wondered, "Could a loving God permit such suffering?"

It didn't add up or make any sense to my little mind. Yet, of course, it wasn't God's doing at all. When sin entered the world and Satan was allowed to roam free, that is when the trouble began. It is he who causes suffering, not God.

Nevertheless, seeing the children so disabled had a profound effect on me. I began to question more deeply as to the cause of their sickness. Some had been born brain damaged. Others had received inoculations that had affected them and so on. The children's ward was as near to a home environment as possible. It looked just like any child's nursery, with similar equipment you'd expect to have at home. The nursing staff appeared kind and loving, but one thing stood out -- these youngsters were institutionalised, and seemingly would continue to be so until their life's end. Why? Couldn't these young people be at home? It was so unfair that they were being discriminated against, just because they were noticeably different. The ones that were considered more able were huddled into the mini-bus every weekday morning, to attend a special educational school, whilst the other, more severe cases spent yet another mundane day -- in the same old familiar surroundings *ad infinitum*.

One day, as I was working on the ward, I had a very strong disagreement with the two girls previously mentioned. I had just found out from the doctors that I was not pregnant again, when I had expected to be given 'good news' and I was therefore feeling low. I had been convinced I was expecting and, when the news came that I was not, I broke down and cried. Now I had trouble I could not handle. I found it too much. I left work that afternoon in an extremely disturbed and agitated state.

Wesley and Gloria were coming to visit me that day, so I was able to share all my emotions with them in confidence. They were kind, but to the point. They thought I was maybe too uptight and too tense to conceive. I had to learn to relax. Yet there was more. Wesley began to speak.

"The Lord is showing me that when you were a child you said you didn't want any children, because of what was happening to you then. Now admit this was wrong and ask God to forgive you."

I was rather taken aback. How could I have said such a thing? I had always been interested in having children. Still, if he implied I had said this outrageous thing, then I must have done, even though my memory of this was completely blank. After Wesley and Gloria had gone I felt like a new person, revitalised and able to carry on with my life.

My period still didn't come, but then, two or three months late for me was quite normal. One Sunday, we were invited for a meal at another Joy's house (Joy was a doctor and close friend of Pastor Licence and his wife, also named Joy). I was experiencing considerable abdominal pain, just as I had with Matthew, but still nothing happened. I remained hopeful that, somehow, I was pregnant after all. I should add that, at this time, I was back seeing the consultant, Mr Harrison, but that he had no wish for me to start fertility treatment again until I had had two normal periods. I had stuck to this regime, although it hadn't been easy. I was impatient to try once more. So, if I had conceived this time, it would have been a miracle. Then to my amazement the miracle became a reality!

I saw Mr Harrison, who examined me before he commenced fertility treatment.

"Your womb is swollen," he said, "I'd like to do a pregnancy test."

"But I've only just had a test," I replied, "and it was negative."

"I'd still like to do another one." he continued "sometimes in very early pregnancy, the test can be negative."

I remembered two years before with Matthew, he had discovered a swollen womb and I'd soon found I was pregnant. Hope began to rise within me and I wasn't disappointed. Yes. I was now pregnant again - with our third child.

Chapter Nine

Another baby

The joy that filled my heart at this time was deep and real. Yet the fear of what the future could bring overwhelmed me. I saw my G.P, who advised me to resign from my current job straight away because of my past history. My conscience would not let me do that. So, I decided to work the contractual weeks' notice. I was excited and thrilled. I had worked for less time than I had anticipated. My work as a cleaner had begun in November and now it was early March. I had been employed for just five months. Everyone seemed to be happy for me, even the ladies who I'd had the strong disagreement with previously. Old issues were forgiven and forgotten and I was able to part with these folk amicably.

I was to take things easy this time and, whilst I didn't find this came very naturally to me, I soon adjusted to being at home.

"O please God," I prayed, "Don't let there be any trouble

this time."

I was in town shopping when it happened. I could hardly believe it! Was I losing blood again? Fear flooded my heart and smothered me like a wet blanket. Once home, I knew what I had to do. I rang the doctor. He confirmed my fears. Yes, I was bleeding, but it was a minute amount. What could I do to ensure the baby's survival?

"There is no secret cure, no magic formula. The only thing you can do is go to bed and rest and hope for the best" he advised.

I was shattered. How could I cope with these fears and pain again? What was wrong with my body? Why was it once more rejecting the longed for child? Why wasn't the G.P. admitting me to hospital?

"You're just as well off at home," replied Dr Emerson.

I swallowed hard, and tried to agree with him.

The bleeding did not stop despite my precautions. My one small assurance was that the blood level remained static and didn't intensify. Yet this had been going on for several days with no end in sight. Once again came the familiar clicking of the telephone and I was through to Dr Emerson's office. It was the weekend and my normal doctor was unavailable. The duty doctor was Dr Ellis, whom I had known from my nursing days. Now I was seeing him as a patient. He seemed genuinely concerned and prepared to hear what I had to say. He was going to send the duty Community Nurse around to see me, to give me a hormone injection in an effort to maintain the pregnancy. I was reassured that, at least this time, they were doing all they could to help me. The nurse came and went and I was alone once more with my own thoughts. Would the injection work? Was it safe? I guess I'll never know whether the injection had any influence over the final outcome, but psychologically it boosted and uplifted me.

It was about this time that I received a visit from Thomas Noakes, a Christian of mature age, who I respected greatly.

"Why?" I asked, as I recounted the whole nightmare saga. "Why is it happening again?"

To my mind, this child had been a miracle child, quite unlike the previous pregnancies.

"Surely," I begged, "God won't stop this pregnancy? It doesn't make any sense!"

Thomas was right to the point. There are just some mysteries in this life that we humans cannot hope to understand. God, in His wisdom, has withheld certain things from our limited comprehension. Job recalls in his time of severe hardship, "*Though He slay me, yet will I hope in Him*" (*Job 13:15*).

"How can I trust him?" my rebellious spirit cried out. "I feel abandoned by him. I am tempted to go my own way!"

Yet, I am sure deep down I knew I could do no such a thing. Where would I go? What could I do? As King David says in one of his *Psalms*, "*If I go over the sea, you are there. If I try and hide in darkness, it is as day to you!*" I was trapped and could not escape. I now had to decide, whatever happened, to trust the Lord and stand in Him.

I am of a nervous disposition, at my core, and resting and enjoying the Lord's peace does not come easily to me. I would have done well to '*Count My Blessings*', as the old hymn says. I think how very easy it is to advise someone how to react when you're not in that position, but how different it can be when you are that individual, striving to cope in some incredible maze-like situation. Yet, we should always be prepared to listen, because sometimes others' advice can be music to our ears.

The bleeding carried on relentlessly and still there was no change. Once again, I felt something had to be done. It came as a great relief when finally I was admitted into hospital, this time by ambulance. Yes, I was returning to exactly the same ward where I had lost Rebekah, as I had now named the child I had miscarried. I had found out she had been a girl and I had felt the need to name her, because to me she had been a real person in her own right. The memories of Rebekah, and this particular ward, unnerved me, but this wasn't Rebekah! It was a different pregnancy. This time, to my great thankfulness and relief, I was near the toilet.

I was in a gynaecological ward, on which most of the patients had undergone an operation of some sort. I had both pain and discomfort but, compared to last time, it was very minor and bearable. I was encouraged to take painkillers, but I felt uneasy doing this in case I harmed the baby. I did sometimes give in to them, however.

This time I had a scan, which revealed a live foetus, and the fact that I probably had fibroids. I found great relief knowing our baby was alive, and appeared normal in every way. As to the fibroids, 'if it's not one thing it's another', I thought to myself! Eva came to visit me and remarked she had heard an old saying that held that fibroids meant the womb was weeping for the children it never had.

"How relevant," I thought. "I just hope the fibroids don't constitute a threat to my pregnancy."

The ward was home to all different age groups, though I guess middle age was the most common. Several women were either waiting for, or recovering from, a hysterectomy.

I seemed to be very much on my own, apart from the odd person in with similar problems. There was one woman of thirty-seven who I befriended. She had never had children and would dearly have loved to have had some. There was another woman who described in detail her sufferings with migraine, for long periods of time. It certainly put my migraine problems into perspective. It had occurred to me that being pregnant had made me more prone to migraine and I was at a loss to know how to cope with this unpleasant condition, now I was expecting again.

The bleeding continued, but remained only slight in quantity and my condition seemed stable. Nevertheless, I was not ready for Mr Harrison's decision when it came.

"I'm dismissing you. You can go home," he said.

Was I hearing right? I was flabbergasted. It seemed like the last straw! I really did not understand and Mr Harrison had left me feeling baffled and confused. Perhaps I should have insisted on getting a satisfactory answer, and on knowing exactly where I stood, but I didn't. It was left to Mr Harrison's junior doctor, who I highly respected, to pick up the pieces. He tried his best, bless him, but even he did not fully seem to have a clear-cut answer. This young man regarded his senior highly and tried to reassure me that Mr Harrison was a very caring person, who would not do anything amiss. I regret to say I can quite easily understand the gulf between doctors and patients when I look back at my own experience.

Paul drove me home, where I was to take life as gently as possible. I was only allowed to get up to cook and had to leave all the housework. One might imagine this to be 'sheer bliss' until you find yourself in such a situation. It can be rather grand at first, to be 'waited on' but it doesn't take much for that initial enthusiasm, and zest, to fade into insignificance.

Helen, my friend, mentioned how her own Mother had to have bed rest when she was pregnant. This had happened twice -- with Helen, her first child, and with Ruby, the last child. She had two other normal pregnancies.

"That's what I may have to do too", I thought reluctantly. "I will do anything if it means having a live baby at the end of the gestation."

Still, I was allowing my imagination to run away with me instead of letting nature take its course.

My family were a bit baffled by my treatment at this time. It was quite plain they did not think much of our Health Authority. I had been allowed out of hospital, seemingly before I was ready for it, and in the beginning I'd had to pressurise my own G.P. to take me seriously. Given my past history, I had expected special, first-class treatment, but my history was apparently being disregarded and, here I was, being treated like anyone else.

It soon became obvious that, not only was there trouble with my pregnancy, but my mother was ill as well and needed a second coronary by-pass.

I think the impact of this unexpected shock hit me harder

than it would have done normally. I just felt I could not cope with yet more pressure. Memories of Mum's previous operation came flooding back. I had been a teenager at the time and had been so immature, so naïve, about the seriousness of the operation. This had been in my pre-nursing days. I had not been a Christian then and had been totally insensitive to the situation. My brother, Paul, had also been caught in this trap, leaving my poor Dad alone to grieve and weep. Only he really knew it was a life and death situation. Poor Mother had suffered a slight stroke, whilst she had been recovering, and some time later had experienced a mental breakdown. Eventually, Mother had seen a psychiatrist in the privacy of her own home. She had not been admitted into hospital for this condition, but nevertheless it had been a challenging episode for her close loved ones.

Now, it appeared the effects of her first operation had worn off, and in order to enjoy the same quality of life, a second one was needed.

What if Mother died? I couldn't be sure of her salvation and that worried me more than anything else. We may be sad when we lose our loved ones, but if they are right with the Lord, what do we have to fear? We have the glorious hope of seeing one another again if our lives belong to Him.

One night in particular I especially remember, I was feeling more uptight than usual and I firmly believe only the Lord prevented me from miscarrying there and then. The phone rang -- it was Frances' Dad.

"I have some wonderful news," he said. "Your mother has given her heart to the Lord!"

I was absolutely stunned. Could he be sure? Normally, Mum and he acted as mere acquaintances and seemed to have nothing much in common. Now he was telling me this incredible news. It seemed impossible. Mum had been so rigid, so stuck in her ways. Could the Lord have used Albert Heath for this great memorable occasion?

"Well, the Lord is a miracle-working God," I happily concluded. "Mother has done the most important thing she'll ever be called to do."

Peace and relief flooded throughout my being. Indeed I shall always be grateful to Mr Heath for leading Mother to the Lord.

Returning to my situation, it was felt amongst my family and me that I should again place pressure on my G.P to have me re-admitted to hospital. After all, nothing had significantly changed. It was eventually agreed that a compromise was needed. I could stay in the hospital through the week, but at weekends, I was to be at home.

A new problem began to raise its ugly head at this time. I had felt so let down and disillusioned by my consultant, Mr Harrison that I was seriously beginning to wonder if I should change consultants. I asked Dr Emerson for his advice. As the other existing consultants weren't to my taste he told me of a new consultant, Mr Clarke, who had just started to operate in the area.

I was in a quandary. What to do? Part of me wanted to remain faithful to Mr Harrison. He had looked after me through thick and thin. Yet, in my hour of need, I felt like he had not been there. Had the time come to make a clean break and make a fresh start? It took me a few days to decide.

My dad was terrific at this time and agreed to pay for me to see Mr Clarke privately. I was in hospital at the time, suffering from a violent migraine. Mr Clarke was great. He did not take any money and he seemed very human and approachable.

Later that evening, Nicola and Freda visited me. I thought I was having the worst migraine I had ever had. I knew I could not take much more of the pain. Mr Harrison's junior doctor explained to me the danger that faced the baby if I was given a strong painkilling injection. In spite of this, the temptation was very real and I almost succumbed to it. The nurses could clearly see my distress and one or two tried to persuade me to have the injection. I was adamant, though. I would resist, but for how much longer?

Freda was straight to the point. Why had I developed a migraine? Was it because I had allowed myself to become tense and not trust God? I knew in an instant she was right, even though I loathed admitting it. I was sick once more whilst my two friends were there. After that, they prayed for me and a miracle happened. The pain began to recede and I was able to get a reasonable night's sleep in the circumstances. Freda also gave me some more advice, which was to learn the whole of Psalm 119 -- something I never accomplished, I'm afraid. Freda's idea was for me to have something to do, during the long months of waiting for our extra special baby.

The decision, meanwhile, as to which consultant I should choose still preyed on my mind. Mr Harrison's junior doctor swayed, perhaps naturally, towards Mr Harrison. I prayed, but seemed to have no guidance from the Lord. To my shame, I did make one major blunder then, and that was to allow reason to cloud my judgment. I felt I had to rush into a decision, rather than give the Lord my consent to speak to me in his perfect timing. So, I firmly decided I would have Mr Clarke. He was about forty, with dark hair round the sides, but rather cropped on top. He was tall, with a twinkle in his eyes. He was very friendly and even called me by my first name, something I didn't mind a bit. I was now on Ward 6, a modern open ward, unlike the dingy claustrophobic ward to which I had become accustomed. The nurses were friendly. Indeed one even reminded me of my cousin's wife, Rachel. They told me of their personal lives. One nurse had been trying to have a baby, like myself. She had two previous pregnancies; now she might be pregnant again. It was finally confirmed she was and whenever I heard she was sick with baby trouble my heart sank. However, this time, good fortune was upon her and she delivered a healthy normal little girl.

Meanwhile what had become of my mum? I vividly remember praying to the Lord, "You can take either the baby or Mum, but please not both. I couldn't bear it." I wanted so much for Mother and the baby both to live and when this happened my heart was full of gratitude. Truly God had answered prayer in a marvellous way.

I was about seventeen weeks pregnant when I felt the first kick. It was terrific and so reassuring. The nurses wanted to listen to the baby's heartbeat and there it was. I could scarcely take it in, for it all seemed too marvellous to be true.

I remembered when I was expecting Matthew, I had felt the first kick at about twenty-two weeks, but with this one, it was those few weeks earlier. This was something that I had probably not experienced at all in my second pregnancy.

Things were beginning to look up for me. The bleeding became less and less and at times completely stopped. I could no longer justify spending the duration of my pregnancy in hospital. I wanted to wait until I had completed twenty-two weeks of pregnancy, since that was when I had miscarried previously. It was a psychological issue for me, but happily the doctors understood and were very supportive.

Once more, I was to be moved. This time, it was to a special weekday ward that shut at weekends. I did not like the ward as much, as it was a typical old-fashioned enclosed ward, but the nurses remained friendly and kind.

I think one of the most upsetting things for me at this time was meeting young girls coming in to have abortions. I am sure you know the feeling. There you are, doing your best to keep your child, and others are mercilessly killing their unborn child. To me, this action seemed akin to wilful murder, and I abhorred it. It seemed the easiest way out of a difficult situation, a way of avoiding all the inconvenience and responsibility that comes with a child! Normally, there was nothing wrong with the foetus. How could these young mothers be so callous and seemingly unfeeling? Clearly my emotions at this time were running very high and, although I don't agree with abortion, I would like to think that I would have more compassion towards such people these days.

I sometimes wonder, if only these people would stop and think, they would realise what joy they could bring to childless couples. Perhaps that would change their minds. Personally,

I do not believe there is ever an occasion one can justify an abortion, except perhaps when the mother's life is in danger. We shouldn't throw a child out just because it doesn't fit in our mould and the expectations of society -- in other words, if it is obviously handicapped in some way.

It was in the middle of May when I was discharged from hospital – not a day I will easily forget. My friend Nicola drove me home.

Great throngs of people were gathering together that day - they seemed to be everywhere. They lined both sides of the dual carriageway, as we wound our way towards the railway station, and past the new hospital. The crowds were waving Union flags. It was a great occasion.

Nicola joked, "They're all celebrating your dismissal from hospital."

I pretended to agree. In reality, the Queen was in Twinmere for the day, opening the new Twinmere General Hospital. I was thrilled to not feel scared any more. The psychological barrier week of twenty-two weeks had been reached and I was free. I felt in my heart that everything was going to be alright. Why, I don't know, but I just did.

I was restricted in what I was allowed to do. I still had to refrain from doing housework and working in the garden. I asked for a home help when I saw Dr Emerson and this was supplied very quickly.

I enjoyed being spoilt. It was nice to be free of the household chores. Ann looked after me. She was a tall lady with dark hair, beginning to grey. Time passed and I began to know Ann quite well. I do not believe it was any coincidence.

She came to me because what she had to say regarding her past was a great consolation to me. Ann had lost her first child, a boy, soon after birth. Later, she went on to have two other children by Caesarean section, and they were fine. She had to work at having her children, but her persistence had paid off. There was hope for me. Then I was given the news that Ann was moving on and I was to have a new cleaner. The new helper was equally pleasant. She was tall, with blonde hair, and had two young children. Her name was Amy and I guessed she was about thirty-five. I had quite a shock when Amy told me she was only twenty-nine. She seemed so mature to me. Amy was friendly with my neighbour Eva. She came from London originally and moved to Twinmere when she married.

It was nice not to be so restricted now. I was able to travel, as long as it was not too far. One Saturday evening, we visited my dear friend Celia and her husband Dave. Their baby, John, was growing up quickly. Celia had been so good to me. Now they were living in a town somewhat nearer to us, it was easier for us to see them than when they had been in Goodwin. I used to travel regularly on the train to see them, but all this had to stop when I had problems maintaining my pregnancy. Celia helped build my confidence by allowing me to handle her baby, change his nappy and wash him etc. It was like old times. But, on arrival home, I noticed I was bleeding again slightly. I felt concerned, but compared to how I would have reacted a while ago, I was mainly calm. I would have to rest again, until the bleeding subsided. I was becoming more used to the bleeding now and recognised it as part and parcel of this particular pregnancy.

Life carried on, and I eagerly awaited our baby's arrival...

At this point I would like to share some of the feelings that I wrote down whilst I was expecting this young child:

1. A real longing to be positive and not to allow negative thinking to take over. *Let me do this first and foremost for God.*

2. A real longing to stop worrying about this pregnancy and anything else that might be troubling me. *Let me do this first and foremost for my God.*

3. A longing to accept any blood loss or any discharge, or anything else that seems amiss. A realisation I can't change the circumstances. I cannot run away and hide, much as I might long to. *Let me do this first and foremost for my God.*

4. Not to be obsessed with my problems, e.g. bleeding, thinking of little else etc. *Let me do this first and foremost for my God.*

5. Teach me to leave my problems with You, Oh God, and not to pick them up again. *Let me do this first and foremost for my God.*

6. *Let me be submissive to You, Oh Lord*, over this child,

much as I long for him or her. *Let me realise this child is merely loaned to us.* It is not ours as such. We have no claim to it.

7. *Let me realise that You, Oh Lord, are most HOLY. Let me fear You with a reverent fear, and have great respect for You.*

8. *Let me not be casual in my relationship with You*, and realise how You detest all sin including mine. *Let me not take Your forgiveness lightly*, realising just how much it cost Your only Son, Jesus Christ. *Give me a heart after Your heart, Oh Lord, overflowing with real gratitude.*

9. *Search me, Oh Lord, help me always to be honest with You*, to be able to confess my own failings without fear, and not to cover them up.

10. Cut out all my self-righteousness, my pride, and my self-ego. *Let me become God-centred, instead of self and baby centred.* After all, I am as nothing. Let me recognise that I have no righteousness of my own, only the righteousness that comes from God.

11. *Let me want You above all else Lord*, for You, the Lord, are a jealous God.

12. Show me what my idols are, Oh Lord, besides the things I'm aware of. *Let me not serve any other God.*

Teach me to recognise that other gods are detestable in Your sight.

13. *In all this, let me realise just HOW MUCH YOU LOVE ME*, with all my sins and failures. You love me, even though I FAIL You time after time after time! When I sin and earnestly repent, *let me know You will forgive me, and cleanse me in Your precious blood.* How WONDERFUL You really are!

14. *Let me realise You are answering my prayers*, though the EVIDENCE might not be seen yet. Haven't I prayed I WILL LOVE YOU 'above all else' with a Godly love, with all my being? Haven't I prayed I will love others also with the love of Jesus? Why do I still feel guilty, that I don't LOVE You enough and others too? *After all, you know my longings*, and You know I can't do it alone, with all the will in the world. It has to be You, Oh Lord. *Let me expect an answer, Oh Lord, forgive me for my lack of faith, also, help me to see that You don't always answer in the way I would like, but You still answer just the same.*

15. *Let me accept others as they are with their faults. Let me accept myself as I am, and be able to forgive myself as well as others.*

16. *If I feel bitter towards You, Oh God, let me confess this and set me free. May I forgive You always though You never sin!*

17. Let me exercise the will You have given me to change. May I realise no one, including myself, can change me. Only You can make me spotless and without blemish.

When I visited the doctor I was aware that I was carrying quite a restless little one. The child was lying in a transverse position. My Auntie Sheila felt that indicated a girl.

"I hope she's right," I thought.

I spoke to the baby quite a lot and said how much I really wanted her. I had heard it was beneficial for the forthcoming child to hear as much of her mother's voice as much as possible.

Later, when I saw the doctor, the baby was in the breech position. I wasn't concerned as I was having a Caesarean birth anyway.

I still attended the clinic, which gave exercises for women in labour. I was meeting other mums and it was something to do, but I felt the granny in the group. I was thirty-two and everyone else seemed that much younger. This time around, I was not quite so strict about religiously attending and really went only when I felt like it. Our babies all seemed due at separate times, mine somewhere in the middle.

September drew closer. Oh, how I wished it were October! I didn't relish another September like the previous two. I had lost Matthew on September 30th and had a miscarriage on September 26th or 27th. I was scared and, to be honest, rather superstitious. People say that 'things run in threes' and in the next breath tell you, 'third time lucky'! Truly, I was in bondage to fear and Satanic lies.

I was allowing my mind to run away with itself. I had lost Matthew, then Rosemary had Chris, who had Down's syndrome, then I had a miscarriage. Would this child be okay? I was failing to be obedient to God's Word, for we are warned to "*take captive every thought to make it obedient to Christ*" (*2 Corinthians 10:15*). We must be continually examining our thoughts and keeping them in check. I know, with me, that this is one of my biggest handicaps.

I had no oestrogen level trouble this time and even the baby moved to be in its right position, waiting to be born. There were scans and yet more scans. "Is this necessary?" I wondered. Seven seemed excessive in one pregnancy. Would it harm the child? Still, I concluded that they must know what they were doing. I put my fears on hold instead of praying about it, as I should have done. I made the mistake of not voicing my fears to my consultant.

It was now about three weeks before the baby was due to be born. I was admitted into hospital for rest. Once again, I was placed on the monitor machine. This time the baby was far from sluggish, unlike when I was expecting Matthew. I observed the heart rate on the machine. The faster rate seemed to suggest a girl. "Great!" my heart exulted.

The nurses were anxious that I should be reassured about the Special Care Baby Unit. I was taken aside by one kind nurse and shown all over the unit. She was keen to bring home to me that most babies in there recovered and went home. It was quite likely, after a Caesarean, that the child would be in the Special Care Baby Unit and it was best I was prepared for this, sooner, rather than later.

The lady I shared with was also expecting her first baby. Her name was Rebecca and she was two years my junior. We soon made friends. Rebecca came from Kirdale and was bright and cheerful. Her baby, unlike mine, seemed quiet and at times Rebecca had difficulty filling in her 'kick card'. This card detailed how many times the child kicked in a certain period of time. Generally, I completed my 'kick card' very early on in the allocated time. Just to let you know, Rebecca had her baby the day after mine. She had a baby girl, weighing approximately 5lbs. 2ozs.

Nicola, my Christian friend, was expecting her fifth child in January. I could hardly believe it. Nicola was about to have five children and I was just expecting my first. Maybe I'd have two one day. That would be enough for me.

"It would be exciting if you went into labour by yourself," she said, "Get it over and done with."

I was not so sure. The horror of what had happened two years previously still haunted me.

I was considering having an epidural Caesarean. After all, I wanted to be awake when the baby was born. I knew a lady who'd had this type of Caesarean successfully, so why not me? Then something happened to change my mind. I was reading about epidural Caesareans in a book, which stated I would still have to push. I was amazed and rather taken back. I had researched the facts. The thought of pushing my baby out filled me with fear and it was a risk I could do without.

The doctor consulted me. I knew exactly the day and the hour I was to have my operation. Wednesday 9th of October finally arrived. I was wheeled into the operating theatre at

8.30 am. It was very different to my previous delivery with Matthew.

It seemed strange being awake in an operating theatre, before an operation. I felt light hearted as the doctors and nurses prepared me for the up coming event. I was catheterised, something I had often done to patients, and now I was on the receiving end. Yes, I was definitely only hoping to have a cut just below the bikini line. The well-known old-fashioned enormous scar of years ago haunted me and my vanity did not want that. I found it a relief to know that the scar would hardly show.

"I'll be glad when it's all over," I reflected. "I just hope the baby will be okay."

Paul had seen me just before the operation. It was a nerve racking time for him too, waiting and hoping everything would go well.

Suddenly, I was asleep, totally oblivious to what was going on around me. When I awoke it was all over. I was in the recovery room and there was Paul with me. He tells me that I was shaking from the effects of the anaesthetic. I was in deep shock. It all came back to me. I was having a baby. Was it alright this time?

"Yes," came back the answer. "We've had a girl and she's fine. She's in intensive care, but not for anything serious. She has a slight feeding problem, that's all."

"Are you sure?" I continued, hardly daring to believe this was true.

"I've actually seen her." Paul returned with confidence. "She's going to be alright."

"Did she come out screaming?" I wanted to know.

"Yes she did."

I was too tired to take everything in as I was wheeled back to the ward, but all I could say was, "Thank you God, at last, for this wonderful gift!"

Chapter Ten

Joy

I returned to the ward, dazed, but thankful it was all over. It seemed to me like the end of some bad dream. My body was physically drained and I felt as weak as a kitten, but my mind was alert. I kept going over and over what had happened. I couldn't rest. This longed for child was ours and she was going to live. It was agreed I would be allowed to see her, but not just yet as I was still recovering from the anaesthetic.

It seemed strange being in a ward where mums were nursing their babies, and mine wasn't there. Yet, this time it was different. I would be reunited with my baby in due course. This was just a temporary delay after all.

I needed to rest and sleep a lot at this time, just as I had after Matthew's birth. But, I was becoming impatient to see our child. Both Paul and I had waited a long time for our daughter, but I guessed I would have to wait still further, until I was considered fit enough to make the trip to the Special

Care Baby Unit.

I must admit when my mother arrived saying she had seen our newborn child, I could not help feeling a twinge of disappointment and envy.

"What is she like?" I asked, probably for the umpteenth time.

"She's beautiful." Mum replied.

Loads and loads of cards, all congratulating Paul and me on our happy event, surrounded me. Everyone seemed to be so pleased for us, sharing our joy. It was a truly happy day for us. The well known saying 'Your Wedding Day is the happiest day of your life' seemed strangely remote just then. This, *this* was surely the happiest day of my life!

Then it happened. I was there in the ward, thinking how happy I was, when I received an unexpected surprise. Suddenly a nurse appeared from nowhere, carrying our child. This time I was bold and there was no hesitation. Unlike our first encounter with Matthew, the reality of the situation seemed out of this world. The little girl was everything I could have hoped for. She had a good crop of black hair, blue eyes, and was very petite in stature. There was no doubt -- our child was not plain or ugly. She had a pretty face. She had a slight mark on the left part of her forehead, which had been caused by the forceps, but it would fade. I fell in love with her at once.

What were we going to call her? We wanted a Biblical name. I had seriously considered naming her Ruth, but now the name Naomi seemed prettier and more exciting, so Naomi it was. Contentment and peace flooded my being. I felt as if I could have cradled Naomi forever.

"How much does she weigh?" I queried, as I marvelled at her tiny features. Everything was perfect. Naomi had all her fingers and toes. I treasured this precious gift. "Normal in every way" I thought happily. Someone told me how much Naomi weighed in kilograms, but it did not mean anything to me. I wanted to know in pounds.

"She's 5lbs. 11ozs." I was informed.

"That is five ounces less than Matthew," I remembered. "Matthew was full term (so they said). Not so Naomi!"

It must have been a good while, but all too soon Naomi had to leave me and return to the Special Baby Care Unit.

I was keen to breast feed, but would have to wait a bit longer before the milk came through, due to the fact I had needed a Caesarean.

Then the crunch came: would I be prepared to get up tonight and feed Naomi as and when she woke up?

No, I decided that I wouldn't. I was very sore and tired from the operation. I had had an intravenous drip in my arm restoring my fluid balance and I felt badly in need of some well-earned rest.

I slept like a baby that night and it was lovely to wake up and remember the happy events of the previous day. I realised that I would be in hospital for a while, after the operation. Now it was my turn to visit Naomi and I donned the white overall to enter the Special Care Baby Unit. I felt frightened and nervous now. A lack of confidence had suddenly hit me, and I wondered if I was capable of looking after such a tiny person, totally dependent on me. I wanted to bath Naomi, but

I was afraid. The nurse fixed the bath for me and I watched her until it was my turn to do my bit. Her eyes were bathed with cotton wool, her hair gently washed. I was taught to wash her below from front to back. The unhealed stump of the umbilical cord disturbed me, but it would drop off in time. After the bath, I had the unenviable task of putting her nappy on. I fumbled and wondered why the nappy wouldn't stick. Perhaps it was because my hands were too sticky from the cream I was using on her bottom. Anyway, the nappy was finally on correctly. After this I could feed Naomi. The bottle was all ready now and I noticed that Naomi was on soya milk.

"Why is she is on soya milk?" I enquired.

"Because we think that's more suitable at present," replied the nurse. I decided they must know what they were doing.

It didn't take me long to become attuned to Naomi's distinct cry. I returned to the ward, tired out after my time with her. This was to be the pattern of my life on the ward -- Naomi, sleep and rest.

I was still in considerable pain from the operation and expected a pain killing injection to solve this problem. This, as I recall, was not encouraged, but ordinary pain killing tablets such as paracetamol were allowed. My intravenous drip, which I'd had since the operation, had now been removed.

It was about the second afternoon that my breast milk appeared. I was being helped by the nurse and shown the right way to breastfeed Naomi when Dr Emerson unexpectedly appeared. I felt somewhat awkward and embarrassed to be breast-feeding in his presence, but Dr Emerson was quick to set me at ease.

"She's lovely!" he said. He seemed so happy and thrilled for me. He was not usually a man to reveal his feelings, so this had a special significance and was something I treasured highly.

The question I had been asked the previous day was now repeated once more. Would I be prepared to feed Naomi in the night? I sighed. I still felt weak and longed for my beauty sleep, but pressure was being placed on me and I felt awkward.

"Alright," I reluctantly gave in. "I guess I'll have to get used to it."

At this period in our lives, Paul was allowed in the Special Care Unit until late at night. Visitors were supposed to leave at nine o'clock, but he was there until at least ten. He was as over the moon as I was at Naomi's safe arrival.

I was fast asleep when the nursing staff wakened me. Naomi was awake and needed my attention. It seemed like some far off distant dream, as I sluggishly made my way to the Baby Unit. It seemed so surreal to be forcing myself awake and seeing to the situation at hand. I breastfed Naomi but, as there was not enough breast milk I also fed her with the bottle. It was with some relief that I finished the feeding and made my way back to bed, not without a cup of tea first, if I recall correctly.

I was fortunate at this time because, as far as I can remember, there was no baby seriously ill in the unit. There must have been memories of Matthew, in my subconscious mind, but fortunately for me that was where they remained. Life continued in this way for a few days.

Diane came to visit Naomi and looked at her through the window -- only parents and grandparents were allowed in the unit. I wondered when Naomi was going to be allowed into the ward beside my bed.

"We've decided that you can stay in the parents' room in the Unit," said a nurse one day. "Naomi is well enough to be moved now, but you need confidence and support and we're here to give it."

I felt humbled at these words. Yes it was true. In one way I wanted to be like the other mums on the ward, but in another way, I felt they were right. I was allocated a pass to go to the staff canteen to eat my meals there. I met another lady at this time having a similar experience to mine. Her baby had been born prematurely and was in the unit. She was coming to visit him, as she had already been discharged.

Psychologically, this lady's presence was all I needed. I did not feel alone anymore.

One afternoon, I received a visit from Eva and her friend, who had helped with my housework during the pregnancy. I felt proud to show little Naomi off to her. I was very fortunate and never seemed to suffer from any of the Day-Three post-natal blues that other women talk about.

I had to have my clips removed before I went home. How procedures had changed since my day! The nurse did not clean the wound with forceps like I would have done in my nursing days. She simply used sterile gloves and got on with the task at hand.

"Why didn't I have stitches that dissolve?" I asked.

"Different doctors have different ideas," was the prompt

reply.

Just a week and a day after Naomi's birth, Naomi and I were allowed home.

Naomi was dressed in a pink woollen frock, which was slightly too big for her. Paul was proud of his daughter and wanted her to look special. Naomi did look pretty and indeed one of the nurses had commented on her good looks. I felt flattered and proud.

Mother was to stay and help out for a fortnight, whilst Paul and I became familiar with our newborn child. It was oh so different than our experience just two years earlier. This time we had a living baby.

Now the hard work really started. I had to make up the bottles, a simple job in itself, but would I get it right? I didn't want to give Naomi too much powder or measure the amount incorrectly. I was a real worrier and doubted my own ability.

Yes, I know it was a sin to worry and all I had to do was put my faith in the Lord. He would have helped me. There was no excuse, but although I may have prayed this, believing was a whole other matter, which my stubborn mind refused to take on board.

Anyway, I prepared my sterilising equipment and the bottles as planned. Naomi had her own room, but during the night I was determined she was going to sleep in our room. Psychologically I felt the need to have her near, and although she wasn't a cot death threat, this somehow settled my mind.

I was determined Naomi's last feed was going to be at nine o'clock. Ten o'clock seemed so late to me, and distinctly unwelcome. I began to get into a routine with Naomi. I was grateful when the midwife came and saw me. I soaked up all her advice.

Every day, Naomi was weighed and assessed. I too was given attention for my own needs. Gradually, I was becoming stronger, so perhaps I should have not been taken back one day when Mother suggested I cooked the dinner.

"Can't you do it?" I ventured. The thought of seeing to something besides Naomi seemed very mundane to me.

"No," she replied firmly. "You're going to have to get used to these things soon enough."

I did not like it, but I knew she was right. I cannot say I found it easy, but as time went by, I developed my own routine. Naomi was a good baby. She was both breast and bottle-fed. After feeding I changed her nappy, then I would speak to her for a little while and after that she would settle and go off to sleep.

Mother left us and went back home. Paul returned to work, and I was left totally on my own.

The Health Visitor took over from the midwife and regularly came to visit me. She seemed to be pleased with Naomi's progress. Every evening, Paul carried Naomi's special bath into her room. I was not allowed to lift just yet, so that was his job.

One evening, Paul and I attended a special Convention at the Assembly of God church. I can still recall the words the lady speaker said to me. She said our daughter 'in particular' would need much prayer. Her next words are still very alive and consoling to me today.

"Your child will be normal," she said.

"Why shouldn't she be normal?" I wondered.

Now, with the knowledge of all that has happened since, I wish I had investigated her words more thoroughly. At the time, I thought I was too busy. Friends, I do believe the Lord does sometimes send other Christians into our lives to guide us, but we can be so engrossed by the distractions of this world that we fail to give them the attention they deserve. Sometimes, we need to ponder and take a step back. In other words, we need to 'watch, listen, pray'... none of which I did. It was with regret that later, when I wanted to question this lady concerning Naomi, I found out that she had died. I would advise you to be on your guard at all times.

Gloria came and visited me. She reminded me about the importance of spending time with Naomi and playing with her. These were precious and happy days. Naomi was still too little to focus properly and I wondered when she would smile for the first time. Most newborn babies smile at six weeks, but with Naomi it was seven weeks. I was assured that it was probably because she was premature.

Naomi saw the Consultant when she was about four weeks old, in the Outpatient Department. Dr Young was happy with her progress and she was discharged from the clinic. I was happy too. It was a relief to know she was doing well. She had her six-week health check up from the Health Visitor, which brought up no major problems.

I also had my postnatal check-up and was seen by the Registrar. Yes, I could have brought my baby along. The medical and nursing staff would have been happy to see her.

The Health Visitor told me that the first three months were

always a busy time in a young child's life, and at four months things would become easier.

It was now approaching Christmas and, like many others, we were wondering just how we were going to celebrate the Festive Season with our young child.

Then the invitation from Celia came. We were invited for Christmas Day and I was thrilled. Celia and Dave had decided Thornbill was not where they wanted to live and had therefore returned once more to their familiar home setting in Goodwin.

We had a quiet Christmas. I shyly went out into John's bedroom, whilst I breastfed. I was relieved when it was over and I was able to re-join the others. John, Celia's son, was just over a year old. He was a bonny baby, quite handsome in appearance, with fair hair and blue eyes. He was quite a mischievous little character. Dave, her husband, was quite adept at seeing to John's various needs.

We came home tired, but happy, and spent Boxing Day quietly at home on our own.

The next day we left to go to the farm, to see my parents, aunts and uncles, to pursue our usual Christmas activities and to open any belated Christmas presents. There were the normal games, like 'Guess a proverb or Christmas carol'. We would work in two teams: one team decided which proverb or carol they would bring into conversation, whilst the other team had to guess which it was. Then there were the Nursery Rhymes, where we all had to draw something that represented the rhyme and then guess what one another had drawn. I can't draw, but still it was fun.

Then it was my favourite. A letter was chosen indiscriminately, as someone opened a page in a book and chose, say, the fourth letter of the second word of the third paragraph. We then had to pick someone from the Bible, say a boy's or a girl's name, think of a town or village in the county in which we lived, name a football team and name a bird, all beginning with that particular letter. Sometimes, of course, the words were easy, but at other times even the most gifted of us had difficulty. The last game of all was indoor cricket. Paul usually did well at this, but I was nothing special. Still, it was fun and then it was time to go home.

When Naomi was three months old she had her first course of injections, but not the one to prevent whooping cough, as it could potentially cause brain damage if the child developed epilepsy. I had suffered epilepsy as a child, so we felt the risk wasn't worth taking. Apart from this, Naomi did very well and seemed to have few side effects from her inoculations.

I was pleased Naomi was supporting her head well and everything seemed to be progressing normally.

I now attended my friend Nicola's church. Paul was not going anywhere and I felt I needed some fellowship. I could not drive so felt in a limbo. Nicola introduced me to Ray Steed and his wife, Muriel. They had started the church, from about four people, and it had just grown and grown. There were a lot of young people there with young children. We met every Sunday morning in a school. Sometimes, we had special visitors. The Bible would term these people 'overseers.' They especially talked about church planting and its importance. Sometimes, I would have to take Naomi out to breastfeed her, but despite this little inconvenience, I always took her to church with me. Naomi was good and presented little problem. The meetings often ran late, and this meant it was not unusual for the service to finish around one o'clock in the afternoon.

Paul, meantime, would prepare lunch so there was always something nice to look forward to after the morning service. I was beginning to lose the little breast milk I had, so after three months, the decision was made to bottle feed Naomi. I was guided by the Health Visitor in everything I did and she helped me enormously.

I always fed Naomi on demand when she woke up in the night. She took the bottle quickly and well. I became accustomed to making myself a drink as soon as she had settled before retiring once more.

I was delighted when Naomi started to sleep through the night. It seemed like paradise. It was around four months that I started introducing Naomi to solids, a little warily at first. I soon found her likes and dislikes. I must confess I did make quite a lot of use of the baby convenience foods. Mutti was advising me to sieve and make up the food myself but it just took so much time. Still, at times, I did concede, and made something slightly different. I would advise any mum to invest in a liquidiser. It's well worth it.

Naomi had lost quite a lot of hair and her hair colour was becoming lighter. She still looked pretty but unfortunately her balding head did mar her appearance a little.

I proudly took Naomi to the local village shops in her pram. I could not get to town in the week without using the bus, so I was totally reliant on Paul to transport us to town at the weekend, or in an emergency on weekdays.

I thought I was coping reasonably well, but there were always the remarks I did not want to hear. Mutti was not afraid of voicing her ideas and was fond of telling me how things were done when she was a young mother.

"Naomi should be out in the garden in her pram," she would suggest. "She ought to be able to look at the leaves blowing in the wind. It is not good for her that you keep her in her room like you do. When I was a Mum, babies were always out in the pram unless there was fog. You can always keep her in the kitchen with you whilst you do your work otherwise."

I squirmed. Part of me felt she was probably right, but another part of me rebelled. This was my child and I wanted to do things my way.

Still, Mutti's influence was rubbing off on me and I succumbed to the pressure. Perhaps she was right and I should be encouraging Naomi to mix more.

I became accustomed to Naomi lying in her pram whilst I prepared the various meals. I quite enjoyed her company and secretly felt Mother-in-Law knew best. I was not quite so sure if I wanted Naomi out in the garden as often as she had proposed though. I found it a tedious nuisance, when it came to putting clothes and yet more clothes on her. Yes, you could say I was lazy and you would be right! Besides, there were some days when it just seemed too cold for Naomi to be outside.

Still, they were happy days overall, and I didn't yet know of the heartache and pain that lay ahead.

Naomi was about three months old when I invited Nicola, Malcolm and their rather large family for lunch. Nicola had been so good, looking after Paul and cooking meals for him whilst I was expecting Naomi. Now was my time to at least try and repay her for her kindness before the arrival of her latest baby.

I shall never forget the horrific story she told me that day. Charlotte, an old teacher friend of hers, had been desperate for a baby. Finally, she had become pregnant and had a baby girl. At first, everything seemed fine. Then, Charlotte started acting strange and seemed very depressed. In the end, she had tried to commit suicide by taking an overdose of tablets. Luckily she had been found before she died, but she now was in a coma. Charlotte was eventually to die from that overdose -- she had received her wish. It was a very tragic case!

The whole thing seemed like a bad dream. Why would a woman so desperate for a baby resort to suicide when she finally had her wish! It did not add up!

I tried to shove the whole unpleasant business aside, but, of course, it was impossible to do so. Still, we enjoyed the remainder of our time together.

Nicola's baby was due roughly in the middle of January, but the child had other ideas. One Monday morning, about ten days later, I received a phone call from Malcolm. Nicola had the baby - a boy. Nicola would be busy, but little Joe (that baby) has given his family much joy and they are truly thankful for his life. Today, Joe is a qualified dentist.

I was not taking Naomi to the baby clinic quite so often now.

It was obvious that she was gaining weight well. Mum's and Tots meeting was held once a week on a Monday morning. What a day to have it! I was always so busy on a Monday.

Mondays had been my main washing and cleaning day for many years. I cleaned the kitchen, the bathroom and did the laundry and I was hardly a quick worker. I could have changed my work routine to another day, but I was set in my ways. I did meet other mums there, but they all seemed younger than me. I felt shy and awkward.

The children played whilst the mums sat and talked over coffee. Gradually, the faces became more familiar and I grew closer to some individuals. There was Caroline with her little boy, Nicky with her little girl and Rosemary with her little girl.

Heidi ran the Mums and Tots Club in the village once a week. Just how she coped mystified me. She was a mother of four young children, all girls and all close together. Heidi has since gone on to have four more children. Strangely, this time the sequence that followed was all boys!

Sometimes Nicola would come and I looked forward to her arrival with anticipation. It wasn't always to be. Nicola was a busy young woman and totally unable to attend every week.

Naomi needed less sleep now. Yet one thing concerned me. She was totally unable to sit up. Some children are sitting up at six months. Eight months is the average age I believe. Yet we waited and waited and still nothing happened. I tried supporting her more regularly with cushions with still no change. It was to be the beginning of coming to terms with the fact that something was wrong.

Chapter Eleven

Something is wrong

It seemed like an eternity to me, but suddenly Naomi was able to sit up. She was now ten and a half months old. She had made it at last! I felt proud and satisfied. Yet she did not seem to be developing the same way as other babies of her same age. She showed no desire to crawl or bottom shuffle like some youngsters. Perhaps she'll go straight to walking, I consoled myself. Maybe she'll be an early talker. After all, I thought I had heard Naomi say 'hello' as her first word when she was only seven months. Nice and early, I presumed. She's doing well.

July dawned that year and with it came an unexpected letter from Paul's old Turkish friend, Baris. He was coming to England and had nowhere to stay. Would we mind providing him with proper accommodation? Of course we wouldn't! After all, he was Paul's friend. I did feel slightly fretful, though. Where was he going to sleep? We had moved Naomi to a room of her own at six months old. Now, at nine months old, it looked as if she was expected to move again, back into our bedroom once more. I did not like it, but felt I couldn't let Baris down.

The phone rang. It was Baris. He was at the railway station. Could Paul go and pick him up please?

My first observation of Baris was that he was a thin, wiry, short man, well dressed in a lightweight jacket and trousers. I liked him.

Baris settled in quite well, but I missed the privacy I had become accustomed to. I found some of his ways rather difficult to accept. He was extremely fussy about cleanliness. Whenever I could, I did his room daily. He did not believe in swotting flies or harming insects.

Baris had a dream. He had set his heart on staying in Britain. He was going into business, and he would shortly become wealthy. I was so naïve at the time that I actually believed he would succeed in his ambitions. Day after day, Baris related his intentions. He was going to work with the big companies and one day he was going to make us rich!

"Marvellous," I thought, "We won't have to struggle anymore."

It was not that long after this that our relationship with Baris began to turn sour. Baris had arrived in July and it was now early September. He had outstayed his welcome.

Originally, we had not set a time scale, but Baris was clearly taking advantage of us. He was one extra mouth to feed and he had no money to pay for his keep. He would promise that 'one day in the future he would make things right,' but eventually we began to see that Baris had no intention of improving his lot.

Our holiday was fast approaching and there was no way Baris was going to be allowed to stay in our house. Eventually, bed and breakfast accommodation was found for our friend and Baris left us. I felt somewhat uneasy. What was going to happen to him? How would he cope whilst we were away?

Paul's sister Barbara had won a holiday to Butlins and she had kindly given this prize to us, which I realise now was a gift from the Lord to Paul and I. In His goodness, He had granted us this unexpected break and had indeed blessed us! Yet how much I appreciated it at the time is hard to say. Paul's mother, Mutti, was coming with us too and I was apprehensive as to how things would go.

It was quite a long trip up to North Wales. We crossed the border near Shrewsbury. It wasn't long before the scenery changed and became more exciting and dramatic. We were starting to ascend a mountain pass. All around, the scenery was grandeur and majesty as the countryside stretched as far as the eye could see. You could not begin to doubt the wonder of such creation. I wished we lived somewhere like this, it was sheer bliss.

Gradually the countryside became tamer and less wild. We were staying at Pwllheli, on the coast. The resort was a mile out of Pwllheli, in a world of its own. After a while we were escorted to our chalet. It was a modest, simple apartment. We had a cooker and a fridge. Mutti had her own bedroom. There was a cot for Naomi and one big bed for us.

"Now to do Naomi's bottles," I thought reluctantly, as I

started to sterilise the container and make up feeds. "This is a chore I could do without," I thought. "Still it won't last forever!"

There were the fair attractions, but Naomi was too young to appreciate them. The cable car was especially welcome. We climbed high above the bay, enjoying the beauty of the sea and beach from a height. There in the distance were the hills and yet further afield was the majestic beauty of the Snowdonia Mountains. There also was a little steam railway at Pwllheli camp, but somehow it lacked the excitement of the cable car.

Sometimes we went out for the day. We visited Porthmadog, where complete strangers greeted me, as if we had known each other all our lives. I had to explain that I was English and totally unable to speak the Welsh language.

Like other people of our generation, we were attracted to the bygone days of steam railway travel, so we boarded the well-known Ffestiniog ride, which runs between Blaenau Ffestiniog and Porthmadog.

Another day we visited the Italian village of Portmeirion, which was on the coast. Portmeirion has featured in different television series, most notably 'The Prisoner.' Mutti was interested in the rocks, as she had recently taken a course in geology. We marvelled at the beautiful china made there, but I firmly decided that we could not afford it!

We visited some slate caverns and were told that the film, 'The Inn of Sixth Happiness', had been filmed there, not in distant China after all. I was surprised and, if I'm honest, rather disappointed. My imaginations of some far off fantasyland were shattered. This was plain old Wales. (Sorry, I don't mean to be offensive to any of my Welsh readers. I love Wales, but I was disillusioned nonetheless.) Of course, film people often alter locations when they're filming. It was good to go into the souvenir shop and see some old-fashioned Welsh recipes and Welsh story books.

I still loved exploring any underground passages. It reminded me of my childhood days and the many Enid Blyton books I had read. Naomi was quiet until the end, when she became rather fractious and had to be taken out.

The weather had been none too kind to us this holiday, and with time running out we decided to head for Snowdonia. We were to be disappointed once more. Paul had climbed Snowdon many years before. Then, it had been a lovely hot summer's day. Now as we arrived at Llanberis we saw that Snowdon was shrouded in mist. Yet there was no going back. We had already travelled some distance from our holiday camp. Paul and I left Mutti and Naomi in the car together. It was not fair on Naomi to expect her to come with us in such foul weather conditions.

Paul and I boarded the little train that slowly wound its way up the narrow gauge railway. Snowdon looked bleak and desolate. There was nothing to see. We reached the halfway point, where we waited for the other train coming down from Wales' steepest mountain. Still, we travelled on, but nothing changed. We arrived at the top, but even then we weren't above the stubborn persistent mist. I recalled the times I had travelled above the clouds in Switzerland, but that was not to be on this occasion. There was nothing to stay for at the top. We visited the shop and caught the next available train down.

Mutti and Naomi had remained patiently in the car waiting for us, two weary travellers.

That holiday, we also ventured to the historical town of Caernarvon to visit its well-known castle. This was where Prince Charles had been crowned Prince of Wales many years before. I loved castles, but somehow Caernarvon wasn't as remote as I had imagined. It seemed to lack something, but I was not sure what. Next time, I decided, we will visit Harlech castle. (We are still waiting). Still, I have visited Conwy castle since then and loved its location. I especially am enthralled how the Victorians built a railway adjacent to the castle, which seemed to enhance the castle even further. Our holiday soon was over and we were homeward bound.

We arrived back to find Baris still had financial problems and it was something of a relief when he left our area and went to live in London.

Naomi, meanwhile, was approaching a year old. Unlike many other children of her age she could not walk. She remained unable even to crawl. This in itself was another obstacle. I'd been to Mums and Tots, and had seen how well their children were progressing. I hid my head in shame, embarrassed, my pride dented. Naomi wasn't making the grade. Once again, I agonised over the reality of the situation. Why does everything that happens to me have to be different than the norm? I was aware of other mothers discussing their children's progress and I felt an outsider. Naomi was different and I rebelled like some spoilt schoolgirl, determined to have her way. I pretended what I saw was not really happening, as if by trying hard enough it would go away. My mother, whom I might have mentioned was well known for her negative nature, tried to prepare me, but once more I shut out her warnings with firm defiance. She was just someone who tended to look on the dark side of things, and I was not going to fall into her trap!

I look back at this time with regret. My non-acceptance towards Naomi's disability was robbing her of the peace and stability she so badly needed. Yet on the other hand, children are not machines. Some children are just late developers. I was clinging to this hope, which I believe is good, but at the same time my mind was entirely closed to the fact there might be something more seriously wrong. It was too painful and something I couldn't accept. I did not want to know. I was not being honest enough with myself, let alone the Lord. Friends, we must tell the Lord how we feel! It is no good brushing it under the carpet.

A week before Naomi's first birthday another step was taken. Naomi started to crawl. I was over the moon. It was another normal stage of development, now happily obtained. I was determined Naomi was going to have a party for her first birthday. I saw it as one way of expressing my gratitude to the Lord for Naomi. I was simply saying *thank you* for this gift. To some people such an action may seem rather strange, but to me it was very real. I purchased a beautiful pink fairy-like dress from Marks & Spencer's. It was expensive but well worth the price. I was proud of Naomi's pretty countenance.

The neighbour's children were invited. Joe made an appearance and Nathan and Christine's young girls were present and Margaret, an old nursing friend, was there with her young boys. My mother had made an effort to come and help me in the preparation of the food. Paul had made a decision to be at home with Naomi, on her special day. The food went down well. The mums happily chatted whilst the children played. They were too young to be into any complicated games.

The weather had been perfect. It was like a summer's day, totally unlike the weather of twelve months before. I felt sad, but also happy. Naomi had reached her first birthday and of that I was thankful.

The following day, I came down to earth with a bang. The washing machine flooded the kitchen floor, swamping the carpet tiles. I was, I told myself, being attacked by the devil. I'd had a lovely time yesterday, but now it was my time to suffer. Sometimes, we give Satan too much credit when things go wrong. Maybe I was doing so now.

Just before Christmas that year, Naomi started to hold on to furniture. She even began to crawl upstairs. I thought it strange that she could crawl upstairs before she could even walk. Rosemary and Gerry let us have their children's baby walker. I was not sure what to make of it. Still, if this stimulated her to walk, that was the main thing, and who was I to argue?

Yet, if I wanted a quick fix, I was to be disappointed. It was to be late May before I had the joy of seeing Naomi take her first steps.

According to my medical records I had not walked till I was nineteen months, although my mother vouched it was eighteen months. Nicola hadn't walked until she was two, there was nothing wrong with her. Another friend, Elizabeth

Goldring, said her son did not walk till he was twenty-one months, although he had suffered from a possible birth injury causing symptoms similar to cerebral palsy. Still, Dr Emerson was concerned about Naomi's late development in walking and it was decided, against my better judgment, that Naomi needed checking out at the local Paediatric clinic. I was upset that they were making a fuss about nothing. Why couldn't they accept Naomi for what she was? Naomi was thoroughly examined at the clinic. A psychotherapist, an occupational therapist, as well as the main specialist saw her. Nothing conclusive was established at this meeting and, as far as I could tell, it was more a case of the authorities now being especially aware of Naomi's condition. There would be a follow up in three months' time.

I did not know what to think and tried to bury any feelings of unease as best I could. I knew it was not normal for most children to see their paediatrician as much as Naomi was doing. These regular visits to see the paediatrician were something I was to become accustomed to.

Soon after Naomi started walking, we experienced the dangers associated with this activity. One evening she knocked her head against some furniture and sustained a cut over her eye. Luckily Paul was at home, and we quickly took her to hospital for treatment. Yet, there was worse to come.

One Tuesday morning in August, I was boiling some water in a kettle so I could enjoy a cup of tea. Naomi was outside in the garden. I should have realised the danger, but instead I went upstairs for a moment.

I arrived downstairs to find Naomi in agony. Her lower

left arm had been scalded with boiling water. She was hysterical with pain and shock. I quickly ran the cold tap over her wounded body. The top layer of her skin had been damaged. I was beside myself with worry and guilt. This time Paul was not home, but Eva was a brick. She kindly gave Naomi and me a lift to the hospital. There, the specific cream for use immediately after burns was applied to her wounds. I had even missed seeing that her left foot had been injured too, so there was further guilt added to my already troubled conscience.

Eva stayed with me as long as she could.

It seemed like an age, but finally Naomi was seen. Would she be scarred? I remembered years ago, when I was cooking at my parents' house, I had scalded my right thigh badly. The scar had faded, and was now almost invisible.

The next day Naomi returned to the hospital, to have her arm and foot redressed. There was even mention of plastic surgery by a nursing friend. Was it that bad? Finally, it was decided there was no need and today, a microscope would struggle to find any evidence of her unpleasant encounter.

Would we be able to go to Germany on holiday because of this unfortunate incident? Would Naomi's arm be healed sufficiently for us to go abroad without any qualms? We still had almost three weeks to go and, yes, we did make it to our planned destination.

Paul had lived and worked in Flensburg in Germany, which is a seaport not far from the Danish border. During the time he had been there, he had met many different people and had many close contacts. When we returned to visit these dear folk, yet more people were introduced to us and so this steady influence of persons continued to grow.

We were staying with people unknown to us previously. They had two children, one older and one younger than Naomi. They were devout Christians and obviously loved the Lord.

They had no television, which I concluded was an enviable situation. They spent the evenings immersed in the Bible and in prayer.

"Why can't we be like that? It would be so nice," I marvelled.

Still they lived in a high block of flats. We had been spoilt with where we lived. We lived in a relatively quiet village, near to a fair sized town. We had access to the countryside, small rolling hills and romantic woods. Yet the town was only three miles away.

I talked about my concern for Naomi with Kim, the lady we were staying with. She was kind and reassuring. I mentioned that Naomi was coming up for two and still not saying much. Kim replied in good English that there was nothing to worry about. I looked up to Kim and respected her, but still my restless spirit refused to be comforted. There was something wrong. I just knew it. Did I thank the Lord for the progress Naomi had made in her short life, or was I too intense in my deep hurt? One thing I know now, I was certainly too self-centred and too Naomi-centred. Perhaps it would have helped if I had got out of the house and found other things to occupy my mind?

Naomi's second birthday came around and we threw her another party. Christmas was fast approaching and I was happy to invite a friend round whom I hadn't seen for some time. Amelia came with two of her three children and we talked over old times. I had first met Amelia many years ago, when we were nursing. I gained the impression she felt that Naomi had not developed to a normal range for her age and that there was probably something 'not quite' right. Yet I continued to suppress my fears. I didn't want yet more pain. I squirmed, perhaps wishing to magic it away.

There were other things too. I had tried to toilet-train Naomi at eighteen months. At first it seemed to work well, but it soon became apparent she wasn't ready for it. I sighed and struggled on, but when Naomi was two and a half, and still not toilet trained, I felt utterly humiliated. I had not worried too much about her incontinence at first, but when she reached a certain age; I did not know what to think. This was the age most children were out of nappies.

Once again, I felt different. I felt a failure as a Mum. I felt Naomi was a failure. I may even have thought God was a failure!

The worst bit for me was visiting close relatives, who expected Naomi to be clean. After all, she was not a baby any more. I found this a difficult time for me. I was constantly ill at ease. She was a girl and not a boy. Boys often take longer to toilet train, but with girls one would expect otherwise. As I look back now I realise that, for the umpteenth time, I was committing the sin of worry.

It was about this time that a former nursing colleague moved into the village. She related to me that her son had been late in becoming toilet trained. I cannot recall the exact age, but it was certainly later than average. Shirley always seemed happy to see Naomi. It was quite common for us to meet up, whenever I took the bus into town. Shirley and I reminisced over old times at the hospital; what so and so was doing now and, of course, close family ties. Her daughter had recently been diagnosed as being a multiple sclerosis sufferer. I enjoyed Shirley's company and her positive attitude, and was sorry when she left to be nearer to her family in Yorkshire.

My friends advised me that Naomi probably would not be able to start Playschool because of her incontinence problems. However, on inquiring further, I discovered another little girl, Sarah, was still in nappies and had been accepted by a local Playschool. This heartened me and I thought I could at least give it a go.

This was a decision I was not to regret. As I was to find out later, the staff at Playschool became like a rock to me. They realised Naomi was different and needed that extra bit of help. One of the ladies, who helped run the Playschool, was a special needs teacher. It was good to see Naomi mix with other children, even if she did stand out like a sore thumb. The other children accepted her, and to them she was part of their group.

There were various activities and diverse goings-on during each session. Each child had a choice to decide what he or she wanted to do, at a particular moment in time. There was the sand and water, playdough, gluing and making new stimulating toys each week. The game choice was continually being reviewed.

Naomi had different helpers, but Sophie in particular took a special liking to her. As time went on, their relationship deepened and a lovely bond was created. It was therefore very sad when, later on, Sophie developed cancer and she died. She was a lovely person and, I believe, through other Christians' prayer, she is now 'with the Lord.'

I, as a parent, used to help out from time to time and soon became accustomed to the routine. Towards the end of each session, there was singing, with hand movements, which brought the singing alive. I felt embarrassed and awkward as the other children seemed to present themselves beautifully, whilst Naomi stood there as a mere spectator. The children's names were read out. No answer from Naomi, of course. One day, I said to myself, one day you will be like other children. Why, oh why couldn't I see her as a gift instead of seeing her as an outcast, someone totally undesirable by society?

Paul's youngest sister married in January 1988. She had chosen Gerry and Rosemary's daughter, Nathalie, as her bridesmaid, and Chris as her pageboy. I felt disappointed that Naomi was not included, but she was still very young and in the light of what later happened to Chris, I am thankful he had that opportunity.

It was about a week before Naomi's third birthday when part of the toilet problem was solved. Naomi became dry, but she still remained incontinent of faeces. As a nurse, I was used to dealing with dirty washing, but I still found washing Naomi's clothes a most undesirable job and was always relieved when it was over. Most children are continent of faeces first, but once again, Naomi didn't fit the normal mould.

We were having a late holiday that year and just before we went away, Naomi became fully toilet trained. It was to be short lived. As soon as we were on holiday, she started soiling herself once more. I felt defeated, but was sure once she returned to her normal environment, things would change.

We were staying at a Christian holiday home, where we had some good strong Bible-based teaching. One dear brother prayed for Naomi's progress and I felt comforted to know people were bearing her up in prayer.

I had longed for another child, but Paul was not that concerned. Our house was relatively small and there would not have been much room. Prior to having Naomi, I had always said I'd be happy with just one. Now Paul seemed happy and content whilst my restless spirit was urging me to give it a go. Even Naomi's new Playschool teacher thought it would benefit her. She told me how another child who was slow had profited from her sister's arrival. My heart ached. I was always longing for what I did not have.

Naomi had started speech therapy at about two and half years old. I was told that her progress would be slow and her speech could take years to develop. The teacher was always kind and sensitive to our needs. Yet, how could she be so sure about Naomi's speech delay? It really aggravated me. Surely God was a God who answered prayer. He would not give me any more than I could bear. In retrospect, I realise I was beginning to get angry with God again. Hadn't I suffered enough already? It wasn't fair! We always seemed to have more problems than other people. Yes, feelings of anger and resentment were beginning to build up. I couldn't understand why it was as if we were being singled out to face heartache and pain, whilst other people, especially non-believers, were seemingly partakers of blessing after blessing. I certainly recognise that the root of self-pity was being allowed to raise its ugly head. If only I had just stopped to listen. Maybe God was longing to teach me something, but I was too trapped in my pain to decipher any such prompting.

Speech therapy continued and Naomi started attending classes with other children who were also experiencing speech problems. If the idea was to stimulate her to speak, it failed. She did not join in with the others and I would come away frustrated and feeling let down. I was expecting too much and totally unable to accept the way things were.

Did I go to the Lord's Word and take refuge in Him? I probably prayed and may even have read daily Bible readings, but was I really looking to the Lord? I knew about other people having wonderful blessings through the Lord. Did I really expect it myself? No. So I struggled on in my own strength, totally defeated and humiliated.

Naomi started to show signs of hyperactivity and, for a while, was on a special diet, but nothing seemed to work. 1989 dawned and I remember that as a particularly depressing year for Naomi.

If I thought things were going slowly before, there was worse to follow.

I had taken Naomi to see the paediatrician and I felt the time had come to be 'up front' with him. I voiced my fears. I had to be sure.

"Is Naomi mentally handicapped?" I asked, somewhat sheepishly, knowing, and yet not knowing. I was clinging on to some hope that perhaps I'd got it all wrong. The words I longed to hear were just a distant dream in my far off imagination.

"Yes", came back the unwelcome reply. "Naomi is mentally retarded."

"How bad is she," I replied, aware of a deep heartache, and emptiness within me.

"She has moderate learning difficulties. Her prognosis isn't good. She may be able to live independently, with some supervision, and take a bath, but she'll never be able to handle money, or marry."

Despite my pain I cried inside that God could heal her! But, though I was saying it, I did not really believe it. My heart was saying one thing, but my feelings and my mind another. I needed to talk to someone. It seemed too much to bear.

The next day, I picked up the phone and arranged to see a friend, Elizabeth Goldring, who had experienced a similar problem with her eldest son, Paul.

Elizabeth understood. We talked and talked. Elizabeth too had been told that her son was mentally handicapped at a very tender age. The prognosis was not good. He would have difficulty tying his shoelaces. He would have more challenges than the average person to lead a normal life.

"I'd like the doctor to see Paul today," she said. Yes, because the Lord had surely answered prayer! Elizabeth and John had moved away from London. They had moved to Twinmere and had managed to place Paul in an open plan school where he fitted in well. However, when they moved to my village, there were problems and Paul was moved to a special school that was geared up for children with physical disorders. Paul continued to make progress and at the age of eleven commenced secondary school. Elizabeth and John never looked back. Paul had done them proud. He was now almost normal.

It had not been easy for Elizabeth and John. They had two younger boys and for a while they had wondered if they would take after Paul. It was such a relief when they had no such problems.

Elizabeth agreed with me. She had experienced hurt and pain, through having a handicapped child. I was not unique. It was alright to feel pain. What a relief!

I came away happier than I had been when the afternoon began. The tears had gone and I knew I could cope. Once again my attention turned to healing. I knew the Lord could heal Naomi. The question that tormented my mind was, when? I wanted it now, before she began school.

It was becoming clearer that Naomi would need some extra help education-wise, something I was determined to use to her own advantage.

Naomi had now commenced nursery education and was there twice a week. She was mixing with ordinary children and with others who had greater or lesser special needs. The only day I had Naomi at home was Wednesday.

Naomi's eyes were checked as I wear glasses. I was disappointed to find out she had astigmatism, something she hadn't inherited from me, but from Paul's side of the family. The eye people wanted her to wear glasses all the time, despite the fact she only had a minor eye problem, so we compromised on how often spectacles were worn. Naomi would later develop short sightedness, but her eyes are quite good overall compared to mine. She can see reasonably well without glasses. I was disappointed to hear from my mother that, according to her sister Jean, the glasses marred Naomi's appearance! Once again, I felt let down and humiliated. The one thing Naomi had never lacked was prettiness. Now even that was being attacked and it saddened me. I felt as if I were being kicked in the stomach. Auntie Jean was also firmly of the opinion we should not have any more children. All such attitudes made me feel almost like a second-class citizen. Mother's other sister, Winnie, could not have been more different. She was kind and always saw the best in everyone.

I started to buy lots of stimulating toys, thinking that might be the answer to Naomi's problems, but, of course, I was buying toys made for children with average intelligence. I was pushing Naomi beyond her academic ability, and it seemed everything I did was doomed to fail. I could not accept Naomi needed toys for younger children. Week after week, I bought different toys, until I at last concluded we could not afford it, and what good was it doing anyway?

Naomi was having one of her hospital outpatient appointments, when it was recommended that she have a special blood test to see if she had a chromosomal disorder. After some difficulty, we managed to reach a nurse from a ward, who was able to do this procedure. The result came back negative. I was informed that Paul and I had a one in ten chance of having a child like Naomi again.

"How tragic," said the paediatrician, "to have such a child? She looks so normal."

"She is normal!" I thought frantically. "Why is it such a tragedy to have a child like Naomi?"

Of course, he was seeing Naomi's prognosis far differently than I was.

One day, I received a lift back from the nursery from a lady I vaguely knew.

"Why don't you have another child?" she asked. "It would be good to know you could have a normal one."

I squirmed, hardly believing what I had heard.

"What's so wrong with Naomi? Why can't people just accept her?" I agonised.

"I'm jolly well not going to have another child for the likes of you," I thought indignantly. "I want another child because that's what *I* want, not because I am trying to prove myself!"

Even the speech therapist voiced her concern for me this way. Part of me agreed I would like another child, but it was not to be. Paul and I weren't in harmony about this and that was that.

It was about this time we received Naomi's statement. It was a fairly long drawn out process. I was fairly ignorant, and did not really understand everything it entailed.

I knew Naomi would probably have to have special education, but I was hopeful this would be within a special unit at a normal school. Yet I did not know what to do or how to achieve this. There seemed no one to guide me or lead me in the right direction. I felt totally lost and neglected by those in authority.

Still, I had felt the Lord witness to my spirit that the day would come when Naomi would mix with her so-called 'normal' peers. I automatically assumed this meant at secondary school. Yet, as I was to see many years later, this was probably referring to the time when Naomi would enter college, and interact within a mainstream setting.

Everything seemed hidden from me. I knew through speech therapy there was a special speech unit in one school just out of town. However, the speech therapist felt it was no good for Naomi. The unit was for speech-impaired children, but Naomi had other problems and needed something more specialised. Now, as I look back, I think the least I should have done is see the Head teacher. All I can say now is, we live and learn.

I was very keen to push Naomi into some kind of schooling early. I was all for the idea that 'the sooner she gets help the better.' There were many frustrating hours spent on the telephone. No matter what I did, no matter how hard I tried, I seemed to be getting nowhere. No one seemed to bother about us and I could imagine the professionals saying in despair, "Not that woman again!" Somehow they managed to brush me aside and the frustration continued to burn within me, totally unabated. I didn't realise until much later that there was more power in writing, and all the time our phone bill was forever mounting higher and higher.

It seemed to take forever, but eventually Naomi's statement was through. She had been seen by an educational psychologist and would have to attend a school for children with moderate learning difficulties.

I knew my mother would not be very happy. She would not be very pleased to know her grandchild needed special education. I felt I had let her down, but what could I do? Absolutely nothing! I accepted my disappointment and tried to carry on regardless.

I believe I made another major mistake at this period in my life, with something I said to the education department. I cannot understand now why I said these words. I imagined something that was not real at that particular time. Friends, don't look for trouble that just isn't there! I did, and we may have suffered the consequences of such stupidity! This was a time to reject the spirit of fear and not entertain my imagination for evil. The Bible quite clearly says, "*For God did not give us a spirit of timidity, but a spirit of power, love and self-discipline*" (*2 Timothy 1:7*). We need to be careful, as there is a great power in speech -- either for good or evil. I shall never know for sure, whether if I had restrained myself from speaking those words, we would have been spared the darkness that lay ahead. The Scripture clearly says, "*Do not be conformed any longer to the pattern of this world, but be transformed by the renewing of your mind. Then you will be able to test what God's will is, His good, pleasing and perfect will*" (*Romans 12:2*). However, I said something like, "What if Naomi's problems are more serious, and she in fact has severe learning difficulties?" The education department tried to reassure me, but the damage may already have been done. How I needed to listen to the tug in my spirit, instead of doing things my way.

I was unfamiliar with the special schools in our area. Eventually, I was told of two of them, but very vaguely. Then, there was the issue of catchment area to overcome. We would have more legal right, if we lived in one area than another, to say which school we preferred for our daughter.

One day, I questioned the lady at the Orchard Grove nursery as to which catchment area we were in. There was no clear response. Ah well, I would just have to wait and see.

Eventually, we were formally advised that there were two schools, one just outside Twinmere and the other in the country.

We started making inquiries. We arranged to see the head at the country school. I didn't know what to expect, but we saw what to the average onlooker looked like a normal school building. I was totally oblivious, at the time, as to what type of children Naomi would be mixing with. When I saw the Down's syndrome children and children with physical disabilities, something inside me rebelled. This was all too much. I tried to accept what I was seeing, but somehow I was not ready or able.

Hindsight is a wonderful thing and, as I look back, I know some of my reactions were undoubtedly wrong. In those days, I was still comparatively naïve about people suffering from Down's syndrome and their intelligence. This was the way I had been programmed to think since childhood. Frances had returned to work and was now working in a nursing home. A young lady with Down's syndrome regularly served the patients there with hot drinks. She had clearly managed to make her way in life. I have since seen another young lady with this condition working in a McDonald's restaurant, so from small beginnings my eyes have been well and truly opened.

We liked the teachers. They were friendly and reassuring. Yet, somehow, when I saw the Head Teacher, I felt there was something lacking. If someone had asked what it was, I could not have been able to pinpoint it, but I had been really impressed by this man's telephone manner and now I was to be disappointed.

"If Naomi does really well, will she be considered for mainstream education?" I queried.

"Yes, but it will take at least two years," came back the unwelcome answer. It was not what I wanted to hear. To me two years seemed an eternity. I failed to see the light and left the school feeling disheartened and apprehensive. Oh, how I wanted normal school for my child. That was what seemed right and natural.

Well, I had not liked this special school, but I could always try the other one, which we did.

The moment I saw the other school I was impressed. Somehow, I knew it was right. This was where the Lord wanted her to go. The school reminded me of a typical, old-fashioned Grammar school from the 1960's. It seemed to have the character of a forgotten era, where normal children had spent long and happy hours. One member of staff even casually noted that Naomi would probably be entitled to extra help from a welfare assistant. I eagerly lapped up such information with great enthusiasm.

Now as I look back with the benefit of hindsight, I can't

help wondering if my feelings led me astray. Sometimes, what seems to be so right is total deception. How could I be so sure and presumptuous that this was God's will, without seeking Him first with every part of my being? Maybe if I had sought Him, we might have been spared much of the heartache that was to follow?

Still, I liked the Headmaster -- he put us at ease, as did the class teacher, although she would be moving soon to teach older children. Somehow, we felt this was right and that finally things were looking upward.

It was still only February and they couldn't have Naomi before September. I was disappointed. Normal children often begin school when they are still only four and a half and Naomi would be almost five by September. Should I have tried harder? Yes, maybe, but I felt weak and entirely at the mercy of the education system. I guess the fight and drive in me had subsided. I was tired of fighting and still more fighting.

The original school could have Naomi much sooner, yet somehow it did not seem right. We had made our choice and that was that!

During this time, Naomi continued to progress well and I was even hopeful that she might have fluent speech by the time she started school.

As I mentioned earlier, Gerry and Rosemary had their own share of suffering. Chris, their Down's syndrome son, had medical health problems and was in need of major heart surgery. He was admitted into Brompton Hospital in London. During his short life, he gave his parents and sister much joy. He had been diagnosed as having Moderate Learning Difficulties, and was familiar with Makaton from a very young age. After surgery, Chris fought bravely on, but his surgery was too much for his tired, worn out body. Ten days after his sixth birthday, he died. His parents later said he seemed to give 'a sign' on his birthday, saying he was sorry, but he could not continue to live. His family were devastated at his loss and we all attended his funeral in Surrey. The vicar who took the service was very pleasant. When Paul and I privately discussed with him the sad things that had happened to our family, he wondered if there was a generation curse on the family. However, as Gerry and Rosemary weren't committed Christians we felt it best to leave the topic unresolved.

At the advice of some fellow believers, who had experienced similar problems with their backward child, I also went to visit our local school. Would the Head Teacher consider having Naomi? She was kind and listened to my request. Yet the answer was to be a firm no. Possibly, if Naomi made sufficient progress in a year's time, she could return to her local school, and be placed in a class one year behind her age. It just never seemed to work out for us, I felt sadly. Yet it seems to happen for other people. Why not us?

1990 marked my Dad's seventieth birthday party, which was a happy time. We were holding this family occasion at the local yacht club. One of our long-term friends, Marion, questioned what was wrong with Naomi. She asked if she were autistic. This had come up before. I answered definitely no. Did I then admit that she had learning difficulties, or try and pretend that all was well? I just don't know, but I rather fear the latter. My pride was involved and I did not want it hurt, thank you very much.

Then there were the comments about autism. I did not want to hear them and I had no desire to be associated with it. Some years ago there had been a theory bandied about by professionals that autism indicated a fear in the mother. Since Naomi had been withdrawn and quiet, I myself (not the professionals) had not ruled it out.

If I had hoped that Naomi's speech was going to improve, I was once more to be disappointed. Suddenly, it seemed as if her speech was levelling off and, if anything, becoming less in volume. I felt so let down. Why, just back in April I had felt so sure, so certain that Naomi would be speaking before she started school. It now seemed increasingly obvious that this was not to be.

We went up to the Pennines that year. Naomi took to the youth hostel warden, Anne. I tried to swallow my pride and not worry what other hosteller's thought about Naomi.

Naomi enjoyed the fair at the Newcastle Metro Centre. Then, she visited the Beamish Museum, where we travelled back in time. I had come prepared if Naomi should wet the bed and, although I had more or less expected it, I still wasn't very amused because the nearest launderette was some miles away. Why couldn't she be dry? I was angry and disappointed at the upheaval she caused us.

Still, it made a break. We were in different surroundings and able to escape some of the pressures of life for a set time. We were away from home and of that I was thankful. Once again I called to mind the hymn, '*Count your blessings, name them one by one, and it will surprise you what the Lord has done.*' Yes, it is true, we can always find someone who is better off than ourselves, but equally it is good to focus on those less fortunate than us and be thankful. We are told in many parts of the Bible to '*be joyful, rejoice always, regardless of the circumstances.*' Yet, instead, how difficult we make life for ourselves! We need to start to see things from God's perspective. What, for us and others, is looked on as a tragedy, is very often the very best thing to happen to us. God knows what He is doing, what He has planned and He longs to rid us of false ideals. Sometimes, our picture of the Lord is so distorted and tainted that we fail to see what the Lord is trying to say to us. I repeat that it had been good to get away.

We moved on to the Yorkshire Dales and I finally got to see James Herriot's 'All Creatures Great and Small' country. I had wanted to see this beautiful part of the countryside for years. Seeing it in reality, I was not to be disappointed.

September finally arrived and with it the prospect of Naomi starting school. I had so many hopes, so many expectations. Yet, there were anxieties and fears too. What if things did not work out, what if we were disappointed again?

I was still failing to see that my hopes were set on man and not on God. It was to be a long time before I finally saw things in a different light.

Chapter Twelve

Painful days

The day finally came. I took Naomi to school myself. The taxi could wait. I wanted Naomi to be confident in the knowledge that Mummy hadn't deserted her and that I was going to pick her up at the end of the day.

Home would seem strange without her. It dawned on me, now, that Naomi was not our 'little' baby any more. She was growing up fast and she was just like other children of her age, only she didn't attend a so-called 'normal' school. I reminded myself that it would come. Perhaps the time wasn't now, but one day my faith would be rewarded!

I now vividly recalled the vision that I mentioned in the previous chapter, concerning Naomi attending a normal mainstream school. I had received this image in my quiet time and just remembering it gave me a reason to hope and not give up.

Nevertheless, at the end of the day, I was brought down

to earth with a big bang! Naomi had soiled herself. Just how this was said I can't recall, but I felt completely overcome with emotion and grief. The people speaking seemed to lack tact and didn't appear to realise the sensitivity of this whole issue. I left feeling humiliated and at fault for the let down. Anything good that was said that day was totally submerged into insignificance as I suffered inside. My heart was breaking and I felt oh so responsible! I told Sarah's mum about the unfortunate incident the next day. Sarah was the child who had had some learning issues, but had gradually caught up at pre-school. Sarah's mother's name was Harriet and she gave me zest and the confidence to go on in the midst of difficult circumstances. We would get there, I vowed through gritted teeth.

It wasn't easy. I saw the head teacher and he mentioned that the teachers were concerned about Naomi's behaviour. She had been unwilling to sit down at the table and had stood on the windowsill, instead of co-operating with the staff. Nevertheless, I felt they were prepared to give her a chance. The headmaster made it clear that it was quite obvious when a child should, or should not be in a special school. It was easy to see when a child would be better off in the mainstream or vice versa.

I was also to discover that having a child at a special school meant I did not become acquainted with the other mums and dads at our local village school. Friendships that may have happened through meeting parents at the school gates were denied me at that time. Strangely enough, it was one of my friends who drew this to my attention sometime after this experience.

When Naomi reached her fifth birthday, we received a report that I found to be very negative. All her bad habits and behaviour seemed to have been over-emphasised and I felt somewhat downcast.

I tried to rationalise my fears. After all, Naomi's teacher had just come out of Secondary School. Perhaps her attitude was understandable, in the circumstances.

Yet my hopes were to be short lived. The school was having a pantomime that Christmas term and the teacher came and took us aside. Naomi was not making the progress that had been expected. She was struggling to keep up with her fellow pupils and needed individual attention. Indeed, in Mrs Baker's opinion, Naomi should be placed in a school more suitable for her needs. It was her firm opinion that Naomi ought to be attending Lynhurst Place, a school suitable for children with severe learning difficulties. As happened so often, I could hardly believe my ears. It was as if the wind was knocked out of our sails. Both Paul and I were totally unable and unwilling to accept what was happening.

When we saw Naomi perform in the pantomime, we felt proud and I couldn't help wondering what all the fuss was about. She was doing beautifully.

It was good to watch 'Treasure Island', to see how well the children were doing and performing in their individual parts. I felt that no one would have known they were handicapped kids.

When the new term dawned, Naomi had a new and different teacher. There was something about Mrs Hamilton that I liked. Her attitude seemed different and I felt she was prepared to help Naomi to the best of her ability.

I began to think my prayers were at last being answered, but Naomi was still having problems. She was obviously in dire need of more attention than she was currently receiving. Yet I had hope and expectation that somehow, given time, she would blossom and I would be proved right in the end.

Any hopes of Naomi having her own individual help were soon dashed. Paul and I felt let down and knocked for six. Thankfully, no more nightmares about Lynhurst Place were mentioned, so I began to feel easier and happier in myself. Surely God knows how much we can bear and He will never give us any more than we can contend with. God was testing my faith, I concluded, and at the right time, happy deliverance would follow. In the meantime we must go through a period of substantial darkness, knowing that the Lord does all things well.

We were in constant contact with the teacher and the classroom assistant, and there seemed to be no cause for concern. Yet, our hopes were to be dashed again and this time beyond repair.

Naomi was seen by a psychologist, as the school were concerned by her lack of progress. What did they expect? She'd not been given the extra help she needed! I was reeling inside and felt totally helpless. It was like watching someone you love suffer and being totally unable to do anything about it.

I tried writing to the head teacher and the education authorities, yet it seemed no one was listening to what I had to say. I had even requested the education authority's attention regarding Naomi having extra help in the form of a welfare assistant, as Mr Roberts had suggested. However, I was to regret my frankness, as it was to seed a poison in our relationship. I had got my facts wrong. It was one of the teaching staff who had said this and not Mr Roberts himself! The education department informed me that Mr Roberts had no right to make such a proposal. I pleaded with this lady not to divulge her disapproval to the head teacher, but I don't think she listened. My relationship with Mr Roberts was tarnished and would never be the same again. I cannot recall being advised not to mention Mr Roberts's name, by the person who spoke of the extra help in the first instance. Perhaps I was so naïve that I did accuse Mr Roberts of saying something that he hadn't, therefore, maybe I should not have been surprised at his frosty attitude towards me. I believe that I was so blinded by my hurt that I failed to see I had inadvertently lied in this incident. This must have hurt Mr Roberts too and I am truly sorry for not seeing his side of the story at the time. Anyway, their mind was made up and I was powerless to have my own way. No, Naomi could not have a welfare assistant for herself. It was out of the question! I was dumb-founded. I was so sure that they would at least listen. Paul also said I had been very foolish and it was not surprising that Mr Roberts was on the defensive. I wish now I had been more wary and tactful and had taken it to the Lord in prayer. But it was too late now. Naomi would be assessed and probably sent to Lynhurst Place and that was that. It was money, of that I was sure.

In the old days, Naomi would have been given the financial backing she needed, but this was 1991. The education system seemed cold and indifferent towards the desires of the parents. Those in authority informed me it had nothing to do with money, but I was convinced I knew better.

Oh, if someone had just alluded to integration in a mainstream setting at this time, it may have made a difference. If someone in the education system had just said to me, "There are other alternatives to Lynhurst Place you know, all is not lost."

One of my friends did know of a girl, who had somehow overcome the education red tape and had been able to get help in a mainstream system. Yes, even in this county, but this had been several years ago, not now. As a result the girl had progressed well and was now considered to be normal. Unfortunately, my friend was always busy and I never did make contact with the girl's mother.

May came along and with it Naomi's assessment with the psychologist. As I feared, it didn't proceed too well and Naomi was given a mental age of one year and eight months. I was told, quite bluntly and without any tenderness, that Naomi was the most retarded pupil at the school. I tried to reason with them and ask what, if Naomi was doing this and that, and had, say, an age of two years and six months, might be their reaction then?

"She would still be regarded as a child with severe learning difficulties," came back the answer.

Oh how I hated that reply. It seemed to have such an air of finality about it. At that moment I think I hated everybody. I hated everyone in the assessment room. I thought they had all failed.

Tears came quite readily. I was in no mood to stifle my emotions. I could not have held them back even if I had tried. Through the tears, I told the assessor I was a Christian and I knew Jesus could heal Naomi. Then the assessor said something that took me by surprise.

"I'm also a born again Christian, but you know God doesn't always heal."

I could not accept this and I angrily defended my cause. Once again, the dreaded school was brought up. I told them I did not want to know. Perhaps I couldn't take in what was said, but to my firm belief, no definite decision was made at this particular meeting and any overall decision was deferred. I asked for information about the meeting to be placed in the post, and as the weeks went by I began to realise once more that what I had requested hadn't happened. As I look back in retrospect, many years later, I cannot help wondering if I should have asked what had happened to the letter I had been expecting in the post. After all, it was always possible it had been lost in the mail.

I let it go and tried to get on with my life. Surely everything would work out okay in the end....

The summer term came to an end. In front of us stretched the long summer holidays.

"See you all next term," I called, little realising that my hopes and expectations of that were going to be cruelly shattered.

I had arranged for Naomi to go swimming with other

disabled youngsters at the Lynhurst Place swimming pool. Imagine my surprise when the organiser came up to me and told me that Naomi was starting school there at Lynhurst Place next term.

"What?" I questioned. "I don't know anything about it. You must have got it wrong."

Of course, I should have inquired further and found out the source of her information. However, I foolishly convinced myself this lady had made a mistake. Surely the Education Department could not do this without our full consent.

We went to Germany that year and stayed in a Youth Hostel. It was good to see people we had not seen for a while. One woman questioned if I had faith that Naomi would eventually attend a normal school?

"Yes, of course," I said, confident in due course that this would happen.

Still there were other signs that continued to be very negative and upsetting. Paul's sister was a speech therapist back then, and her work colleague had recently moved from Surrey to our region. This lady also seemed to know that Naomi had been moved from her old school to Lynhurst Place. How on earth did she know this? I then proceeded to put my head firmly in the sand, yet again, and chose to think the lady had been misinformed, instead of checking it out in a sensible manner.

We arrived home from our holiday only days before the beginning of the new school year. We were going through the post, as one does after a time away. As I opened the mail, I came across a letter that left me numb with shock and disbelief. It was from the taxi firm, saying that they had arranged for Naomi to travel to Lynhurst Place from our home. To say we were bewildered and totally lost in confusion was an understatement. I tried to understand, but couldn't. I can only reiterate what I said previously. I am of the persuasion that any letter sent to us concerning this matter must have gone missing in the post. At the meeting in May, it had not once been made clear to me that this was definitely the outcome of the meeting. We just did not know what to do. I did not want my child to attend a school for children with Severe Learning Difficulties when, to our mind, this label seemed absolutely ridiculous for Naomi. I consulted my friend Helen. She might know what to do. Under her guidance and direction I wrote to the education authority. I explained that my husband, Paul, had never been consulted regarding the local education authority's decision to send Naomi to Lynhurst Place. This was something they couldn't deny! Somehow, they waffled their way out of the situation and stringently justified their cause. I was slipping fast.

The day came for Naomi to start school. Guided by Helen, she did not attend. Paul had managed to have some time off work, so after contacting Spitalfields School Governors, we arranged to meet one that very afternoon. Perhaps we should have waited, because I think the person we saw was an emergency fill in and not the most suitable individual to hear our case.

However, we felt we were doing right at the time, and were keen not to keep our daughter off school for long.

We were ushered into Mr Roberts's office, where a lady

in her fifties greeted us. She had long grey hair set in a bun. We had expected a sympathetic hearing, but were sadly mistaken. This lady meant business, but not in our favour. I tried to enumerate Naomi's positive points. Her speech was improving, her behaviour also and, to my mind, there had been good overall encouraging signs of real progress. I might just as well have talked to the wall. Naomi needed more than speech, came back the unwelcome reply. She was severely retarded and could not get the help she needed at her present school. As the conversation continued I tried to get the lady to see our point of view, but it was obvious that we were totally on our own and she just seemed to be washing her hands of any responsibility towards Naomi. We were up to our necks in deep water and we knew it.

We had tried so hard, but the battle was lost. We were defeated. I went to say goodbye to the teacher and her classroom assistant who I especially liked. They assured me it was for the best. If Naomi remained in her present environment, she would drop further and further behind. Now, she would get the help she needed and progress would surely come. As I talked, tears freely flowed. I felt a total failure! What must they think of me as a mum? What a mess I had made of things! Would I visit them in the future? I assured them I would, but I'm afraid I broke that promise.

That same afternoon, Paul and I finally saw the dreaded Lynhurst Place. Her new headmaster, Mr Owen, was reasonably young and, to me, looked Mediterranean. He was short, of medium build and had dark hair and eyes. I was not sure, but I felt I liked him. Her new teacher, Marion, struck me as being a quiet person and again I was undecided whether I liked her or not. Mrs Hamilton had been so natural. This all seemed so strange and I did not know what to think.

Naomi would be in a group of eight children. Paul and I wanted her to get one to one help, if she was attending a school such as this. However, as expected, the reply was that this would just not be possible. Nothing I wanted seemed to be happening. It was all so unfair! What sort of standard would she be in her class? There would be a mix of brighter and less able children was the unwelcome reply.

"We'll see about that," I gritted my teeth.

"Sometimes pupils do really well here!" Mr Owen replied.

Clouds of darkness seemed to engulf the three of us in a fiery furnace, and there was no escape! I think this was one of the saddest and most unbearable times in our lives. As far as I was concerned, God had abandoned us and no longer seemed to care. It had been one thing after another and now this. What on earth was God doing? Where was He in all this?

I poured out my heartache and pain to Nicola and her friend, Freda. To me, Lynhurst Place was the end. There was no hope for Naomi now she was there. I might as well give up and accept the fact. Then Freda said she'd had a mental image of me trudging through the snow. There were various paths I could take. Right at this point in time, I was to take one particular path, but eventually other steps would become apparent.

I had become so muddled and confused. I had been so sure Spitalfields was the right school for Naomi and now this. Was it possible I had got it so wrong? Had I been so blind to all that the Lord was trying to show me? Even now, with the dawn of another chapter about to emerge, might I be able to look back and realise the pain had not been in vain?

Chapter Thirteen

Lynhurst Place

Time went by and I began to see that not everything was hopeless. The Lynhurst parents held regular meetings at the school and, through this, I realised I was not alone. The first meeting I felt I was simply an onlooker. It was as if I was viewing events from another planet and somehow nothing was quite real. The parents and carers were friendly enough, but getting to know them represented something extremely painful.

We were all there because we had something in common and I did not want to acknowledge it. They represented reality and I, as usual, was trying to convince myself this could not be happening to me. Naomi was not part of their 'category'.

I can honestly say, though, that I never felt like that again on subsequent meetings. Perhaps the Lord was beginning to work on me too.

Yet, there were still issues. I felt uncomfortable about

confronting my parents with the 'unpleasant truth.' I had always told them everything and this seemed like a betrayal. It wasn't so much the case with my father. He would understand, but Mother was a different matter. Her pride bothered me. The feeling that we had somehow 'let her down' was already making me tense. I just felt Mother could not handle this news, that it would be too much for her to bear. Strangely enough, I did tell my cousin Stuart, possibly because he is a teacher. No other member of the family knew. Over a period of time, though, this secret did come out into the open. I can't remember when exactly, but I believe it was at the right time.

There was good news for Naomi at last, so that was the Lord's intervention. Her rating in the classroom had changed. She was no longer seen as the most retarded child in the class. No, she was now viewed as the most able and this gave me reason to hope. Whilst in class she was mixing with children with little or no speech, but during playtime she joined older, talking children. So, no, it wasn't all bad. The behaviour was something that could be worked on, and worked on it would be.

December 1991 came and with it the return of a popular figure from the past. Reverend Reginald Ashby, as I mentioned previously, had lived in France for several years and, together, he and his wife Audrey had pastored a church. Reg, as we knew him, had lost his dear wife to cancer in June. He now felt a calling to return to England, with the view to possibly shepherding our little flock. It was great to see him and introduce him to our daughter again. Yes, he had faith -- Naomi could be healed. Suddenly, I no longer felt alone. I wasn't mad for believing it was possible. Here was a man of God who was willing to express his views on the subject and I was comforted.

I often have the impression that, whilst we may have faith in physical healing, when it comes to the brain, that's somehow different. Why is this? I am mystified. As I see the matter, whether it's a psychiatric illness or a mental disability, either way, we're trumped. What's wrong with us, folks? God is a God of miracles and I don't believe He's restricted to physical healing either! The way I see it is this, if we don't expect miracles to happen, then they are not going to come to pass, are they? Looking into Acts in the New Testament, miracles were an everyday occurrence. Did they stop happening after the great apostle Paul died? No, a thousand times, no! But we do need to get back to a simple, childlike faith, where we do not doubt, we do not reason. The majority of believers do not really anticipate miracles or healing today. How sad! Then there are the counterfeit miracles. Yes, you've guessed it. Satan can heal too, so we have to be careful. I have said to the Lord, "Let there only be healing if it comes from You, Lord, there is no way I want healing at any price."

Still there were times when I did not feel at one with the church. There were those who genuinely and lovingly, as far as they could see, tried to tell me it might not be God's will for Naomi. She continued to do well at school, but it wasn't an ideal situation. Now she was the brightest in her class and, unfortunately, there was not a more able child there for her to relate to.

It was about this time I began to 'take to' Naomi's teacher

Marion and a special bond between us was formed. Marion was a Christian. She did not feel the same as I did about healing, but in other ways there was a union. She loaned me a book about a Down's syndrome child that came from a Christian background. I found it helped, but somehow there seemed something lacking. I think one of the problems I have had to face is the fact that Naomi is our only child. If I had had a so-called 'normal' child, I think I would have been able to have a more balanced take on life. Being willing and able to accept Naomi would have been so much easier. This young girl had two normal brothers and so, yes, I still felt alone. I have been told, and no doubt it is true, that having other children can also present problems. I will give some examples. They can be teased by their friends, and other biased youngsters. They may feel Mummy and Daddy do not love them as much as Harry. After all, he receives far more attention than they do. Children may indeed feel jealous and resentful and it is important that they know that they are loved just as much as their disabled sibling. Much wisdom is needed to nurture the 'normal' children and time alone with them is invaluable. Yet for me, of course, this wasn't the case and I needed to really believe *Romans 8:28*, "*All things work together for good for those who love God*" (*New American Standard Bible*). At last, I think I was really trying to see things from God's point of view, no matter how painful it appeared.

When Naomi reached the age of seven, new milestones were attained. Naomi finally became completely continent, her speech was progressing well and she was beginning to use sentences. I could recall a few years earlier when a friend of ours, a Christian doctor, had said that Naomi might never speak. I am sure she would be glad to have been proved wrong. We were also made aware at this time of the possibility that Naomi might need Makaton, which is geared towards children and adults with little or no language use. Paul and I had reluctantly gone along with this. I had attended a session of learning this way of communicating with Naomi, but deep down both Paul and I knew it was not necessary in her case. Given time, we were proved right. We had much to be thankful for and it was good to know Naomi could communicate normally.

It was also around this time that I said something rather unwise to a close friend and I would say now, be wary what you say to others -- they may not react in the way you are expecting! I was very familiar with my mother's thoughts on my association with Paul. She did not regard either of us as that intelligent. The response still came as a shock, however, when I asked this other person whether they thought that Paul and I had a disabled child because we were not that bright ourselves. They seemed to insinuate that this indeed could be the case. I was immediately overcome with thoughts of inferiority and did not know what to think. However, I would say now, get into God's Word and let Him transform and renew your mind, as discussed in *Romans 12:2*. I now know of doctors and solicitors and other gifted people, who have produced disabled children. Also, if we are not careful, there is a danger that we can blame God for our lack of intelligence. I believe we will all be accountable to the Lord for what talents and gifts He has given us, but not responsible for what is perceived as not our gifting. It is up to each one of us to discover and use these gifts in an appropriate manner for God's glory.

A few months after Naomi had started at Lynhurst Place, a young boy named Simon was admitted to her class. It soon became clear that Simon's learning difficulties were only mild and that he was merely a late developer. He went on to bypass the other special schools in our area and attend mainstream school.

At the opposite end of the spectrum, there was a young girl suffering from a rare genetic disorder called Retts Syndrome. This is an illness that usually only affects girls and it is very debilitating! The child develops normally until she is about eighteen months. Then the child either fails to make progress, or she regresses. Even if the child had started to walk or talk, this comes to an abrupt end. It is very sad! A former nurse adopted the child, who I will call Amy. She was in a wheelchair and had a special tube to feed from. Her outlook for the future was very bleak. She was expected to die in her teens. (I have recently been informed that there is a mild version of Retts Syndrome, but I cannot verify this).

Zoe, another mum at the school, had a son called Adam who suffered from a different rare genetic disorder. Adam was extremely 'over active' and never seemed to tire. He seemed to be on the 'go' 24/7 and only slept for about two hours at night. My heart went out to Zoe and her family. At least Naomi slept well at night. I had much to be grateful about. Thankfully, Zoe was able to have regular respite for Adam.

I found that another of the mums had given birth to a daughter with Down's syndrome when she was only nineteen. It was an eye opener to hear this, as I formerly had been of the opinion that it only happened to older women. Fortunately this girl went on to have other children who were perfectly normal.

Outside school, there was an occasion when the family were gathered together. All the other children were playing happily alongside one another. Naomi remained in her own little world and I felt sad. She still was not mixing well. Some days later, I received a lovely letter in the post from my Aunt Amy. It was psychologically uplifting. In the letter, Aunt Amy wrote she had a strong feeling that Naomi was going to be 'fine' as an adult. I have never forgotten this kind gesture. Aunt Amy was a Christian. Maybe she didn't hold exactly the same beliefs as me, but I found her letter comforting and reassuring. I think I told her this before she died. I hope so.

At the end of January 1993, Naomi saw a psychologist that she hadn't seen previously. She had a heavy cold and was hardly at her best. Yet the school was happy she had made good progress. She now seemed to have an age of between two years eight months and two years ten months, something I was supposed to be happy about. Since she was six years old at the time, I found it hard to be exactly thrilled, but yes, I was encouraged. There seemed to be a totally different attitude than had been at Spitalfields School.

Over the years Naomi had many taxi drivers, most of whom she related to well. Naomi also had many different escorts and, when she was about eight or nine, had a new companion -- a young boy of Indian origin. He suffered badly from epilepsy, was incontinent and was confined to a wheelchair. Later I found out he had suffered brain damage around the time of his birth, but his twin brother was fine. He regularly had respite care, in order to give his family a break. Some professionals suggested we tried this for Naomi, but we were against it. Paul and I did not like the idea of Naomi continually mixing with disabled youngsters. After all, at school, she was surrounded by 'special needs kids' all day long. We continued to want her to socialise with 'normal kids' as much as possible.

Although we did not welcome Naomi going into respite care, there were other options that our social worker informed us about. We heard about shared care that involves disabled youngsters going into a normal family setting and socialising with them. This gives the carers a well-earned rest. We were well aware there was a long waiting list for this service. At this time we became acquainted with a Christian family that had a teenager aged eighteen and two younger children. Years ago, they had looked after people with special needs and were considering doing it again. The husband was training to work as an occupational therapist for people with learning difficulties at a local hospital. The hospital is now closed. Over a period of time, we saw these people regularly, but eventually it fell through, possibly due to work commitments.

Anyway, after a while we tried again. On this occasion, the people involved were not Christians and lived in Whitedale, a few miles away. The family had twin girls who were already involved in looking after a young woman with a physical disability. I had my reservations. The girls were only eleven years old and were younger than Naomi. I felt that taking on Naomi as well as the person they already had might be too much. It took a few months for my suspicions to be confirmed and we were no further forward. Yet again we tried, and once more we were to be disappointed. This time the person was a single lady in her thirties. We would have preferred a family, so this situation was far from ideal. Anyhow, we agreed to give it a go. She had Naomi a few times and did her best to entertain her. By then, Naomi was fifteen years old and this carer had wanted a much younger person. Paul thought the reason the woman stopped having Naomi was that we did not use her enough, but somehow that did not ring true to me. Eventually, we forgot the shared care idea. Happily, our experiences aren't necessarily that common.

I was feeling that Naomi should be given a chance to be considered for mainstream education. Gradually, it became plain that I was not on my own here and I was privileged to meet the Colemans, a young couple who fully believed in integration. Their daughter, Lorraine, was another pupil at Lynhurst Place and the eldest child of three (it is now four). Lorraine had little speech, was still incontinent and had a physical disability which affected her legs, but they were going to do all they could to help Lorraine. They were determined to fight tooth and nail for her. So far, however, it had been far from plain sailing.

Lorraine had started at a local primary school on a trial basis. It seemed at first that things went well. Yet, unfortunately for the Colemans, the local press had twisted their story and now they were having trouble with the head teacher there. Lorraine's once a week visit to the primary school had become strained and it was obvious she was no longer welcome there.

Over a period of time an integration group was formed and we began to meet on a regular basis. Yet, even here, it was difficult to convince other parents of disabled children to attend the meetings. We saw the same familiar faces, but as for new ones, it seemed like reaching for the moon. I stand amazed now, when I see parents who firmly believe the authorities know best. Their children have special needs; therefore they should be taught in special schools. I can understand this viewpoint, but is this how Jesus would treat these people I ask? It almost seems to suggest 'lock the door and throw away the key.' These children are not a menace to society. Indeed, just to reinforce what I have said before, I have been horrified at some Christians too. They too appear to be far from understanding and, they happily go along with what I believe to be an out-dated system. I feel very strongly about this. I wanted my child to be treated as a normal human being. Still, that seemed to be a 'far off' dream. She remained isolated in her secluded world. Naomi and others like her are dealt with differently by segregating their education. What have we to fear from such people? Is it just an excuse or a prejudice from generation to generation? Our Lord loves us just as much, whether we're bright, average or have learning difficulties. There are no second-class citizens. If God loves us like that, what right have we to lay down such harsh inhumane rules? How He must weep at man's inhumanity to man!

Trying to get Naomi integrated into a normal mainstream setting, just for an afternoon a week, proved far harder than I could have imagined.

It soon became perfectly clear that the Headmistress at our local school was very sceptical and out-dated in her outlook. I received a letter in the post outlining the reason for her refusal to have Naomi, even on a trial basis. The reason: Naomi could not cope with understanding concepts such as the Victorians and the Romans. Well, obviously this was way beyond Naomi's understanding, but Mrs Wilson made this appear the most valid argument. Once again, I was staring defeat in the face.

Where do we go from here? Why do we have problem after problem? I wondered whether, if we lived somewhere else, Naomi might be treated with more justice. Unfortunately, we live in a county that is well known for being somewhat restrained with their education budget. It seemed all too hopeless. What could I do? Moving was out of the question. Paul's job was as secure as any job could be in these hard economic days, so to move, unless it came from the Lord, was folly.

My search led to a nearby private school. It was Christian in origin, and I hoped would lead somehow to a more normal environment for Naomi. They agreed to have Naomi on a trial basis every Monday afternoon. An assistant, who normally helped out on Monday afternoons, would have Naomi as an extra and give her one-to-one help whenever possible. I was to go along, but not stay in the classroom.

Sadly, life is never dull with a handicapped child and Naomi had recently reverted to wetting herself which put extra pressure on me, as I would have to remove her from the classroom and struggle outside to a Portakabin, where the toilets were situated. I was so disappointed. Why did this have to happen just now? It wasn't fair! The next two times Naomi was allowed to use the staff toilet, which was nearer.

The staff were pleasant, but perhaps honesty was somewhat lacking. I say this because one morning a letter arrived in the post. The school was unable to have Naomi any more. She had outstayed her welcome by standing on the teacher's desk and throwing chalk and other objects about. She would have to go.

I was absolutely shattered. In hindsight, the school probably had voiced concern over Naomi's behaviour but I had failed to hear it. I saw the situation differently. Why hadn't the authorities warned me at the time that the last time we had attended the school would probably be the final occasion? I wanted to retaliate, write a letter or perhaps make a phone call. I was both choked and mad at the same time. It felt like God had let me down again. I don't know how I survived this setback, but my Christian faith gave me hope that she would get on better next time. The school situation was to remain on hold for another twenty months, so I lost contact with the school. I was grateful that they had at least said they would remember us in prayer.

Naomi learnt to use the trampoline and gained confidence in that activity. The ladies who ran this class happened to live in my village and were truly dedicated teachers. It was a shock then, after only two years, to be told that funds for this class were no longer available. Everyone was upset and, for the teachers, it was time to move on.

Lynhurst Place was also very good at ensuring their pupils could swim properly. Naomi learnt to swim and, today, is a stronger swimmer than either Paul or me. She used the swimming pool at her school at first, but as her skills developed, she went to the local town's swimming pool with other youngsters from her class. This was not the only physical activity for Naomi and her classmates; they also attended riding lessons, especially aimed at people with disabilities. Riding helps improve co-ordination and stimulates the child to learn. After about two years, riding was stopped in favour of helping the young people learn different and new skills, but just before leaving Lynhurst Place Naomi did take up her riding once again.

Naomi even had private riding lessons at a local riding school for a brief time. After a while, she moved further afield to another riding school with supposedly more 'one to one' help. We met a woman there whose daughter had mild learning difficulties. The mother shared with us that her blood group was Rhesus negative, whilst her daughter was Rhesus positive. She wondered if this had affected her daughter. Like this mother, I too am Rhesus negative and had to have an injection because of it sometime after my first pregnancy, but cannot exactly recall when. Did this contribute to Naomi's problems? I doubt it as most people with this condition go on to have healthy babies.

Naomi also went to dance classes in the village for a

while. It was good, knowing she was being well catered for, and I appreciated Mrs Evans' kindness which did encourage me. I still continued to have niggles of jealousy, though. For instance, I felt sad that her cousins and my friends' children could perform in pantomimes in their local community -- a dream that just wasn't realistic for Naomi.

Naomi and I often went on walks and bicycle rides at the weekend and these continue to this day. She made friends with a local farmer, who I will call Colin, and a farm worker named George. Unfortunately George died a few years ago at a relatively young age. Naomi especially enjoyed seeing the cows being milked. It appeared to be a novelty to her.

It is so easy sometimes, to be overcome by the dark things in life. There were surely occasions when God showed his Almighty arm of protection and kindness to us as a family. One day Paul had invited his sister, Helen, and her husband over for the day. We were seeing to them and giving them attention, as one does, when we realised Naomi was missing and her bicycle was gone too. You can imagine the upset. Where was she? We weren't sure, but it seemed possible she had gone to visit Colin at the farm, which was about a mile away. There were relatively busy roads nearby and to say we were worried was putting it mildly. We went to the farm only to be disappointed. Paul then decided to try the local children's playground. I believe now that this was the Lord's intervention. We found her there, safe and sound. It was such a relief to have Naomi back, none the worse for her experience.

Naomi moved up a class and I missed Marion. Somehow

the rapport that had existed between Marion and I ceased when Naomi had a new teacher called Elaine.

Elaine was an older lady in her fifties with very deep-rooted beliefs and a strong hold on her traditional, old-fashioned views. Nevertheless, we were on amicable terms and I regularly went to see how Naomi was progressing.

After some time at the Pentecostal Church, we returned to the Assembly of God. The church did not have its own Sunday school then. Yet, at least we managed some integration, albeit very small, and Naomi was able to attend the nearby Methodist Church for her Sunday school teaching. Over the years, she made good progress there, and the other children seemed to accept her without any problem.

It was at this time that I met Marie, a French lady living in England with her American husband and four children. Marie's husband is Jewish. Marie and I bonded well together and had a lovely relationship. We shared everything. She was there when I needed her and I would like to think that I was there for her when she needed me. Marie is a very kind, sociable person with a heart of gold. She is an extremely busy lady and I rarely see her now, but I believe the Lord sent her into my life 'for a season'.

Naomi also went to Girls Brigade every Friday evening, where she mixed with normal children and, yes, disabled ones as well. Still, I wanted more.

There was a meeting with Mrs Wilson again, where it was finally agreed that Naomi could attend an after school activity, a sewing session, at the mainstream school. To my mind, this was ridiculously unsuitable. She needed to do something to let off steam. In addition, if she took after me she would be hopeless at sewing anyway! I tried to persuade the authorities to think again, but my views were totally ignored. Naomi started attending the sewing class with a welfare assistant and I was hopeful something good would come out of my efforts.

Amanda did her best and, to start with, all looked well. However, Naomi was unable to make friends and the only children who took to her were youngsters who we vaguely knew from before.

It was not long before the unwelcome news came. Naomi was excitable and letting off steam. She seemed to take great pleasure in being naughty and disruptive. Bang went the sewing needles, all over the floor. The quiet class was quiet no more. She even ran out of the class on one occasion and started screaming. Naturally such behaviour was totally bizarre to the normal children and they did not like it. Amanda, bless her, did her best, but Naomi had won.

I frantically tried to change people's minds, pleading for just two more chances! Unfortunately, I was told that some of the children were now refusing to go to needlework anymore, because of Naomi. I felt awkward and longed to hide my face in shame. Please, let it not be so!

But after all, I could understand the children's and their parents' points of view. Did they all feel like that, though? Surely not! Yet though I tried to believe this, there was doubt in my heart. It was fairly obvious that there had never really been any willingness to have Naomi anyway. Of course, I accept that her behaviour was unacceptable in every way.

However I cannot help wondering whether, perhaps, a more sympathetic school may have produced a different outcome. My wonderful father felt for me especially. He was right behind me all the way. His only concern was Naomi's behaviour. That had to be rectified if we were to have any chance of accomplishing our goal.

Still there had been progress in other areas of inclusive therapy. Although we had tried in the past, the local Brownies group previously had not accepted Naomi. However, the Guide Leader now allowed her to be part of the group. At first, Naomi's time at the Guides seemed to be a positive thing, but after about ten months it came to a sudden end. Her behaviour was still unpredictable at times and, one day, she exposed herself by pulling down her clothes, thereby revealing a dirty menstruation pad. It was all very embarrassing! I felt humiliated and ashamed. I had been hoping Naomi would make some new friends through this experience, but it had not happened. Naomi had also decided Girls Brigade was no longer for her and that she would rather stay at home and watch 'Top of the Pops'.

It was not long after this that my dear, kindly Dad was taken ill. At first we had thought it was something straightforward like a hiatus hernia. Sadly, I was soon to experience a major upheaval in my life. For once, the pain was not surrounding Naomi, but other people I held dear.

Chapter Fourteen

School days continue and deaths in the family

In the July of 1994, Dad had major surgery. By now it was known that something more serious than previously thought was wrong. Dad had to have an exploratory operation and I shall never forget hearing the devastating news when my brother Paul rang! Dad's cancer was much more advanced than any of us realised. The picture communicated was grim. We were informed that he probably only had two or three months to live. Dad was yet to awaken from the exploratory surgery. When he woke, he was going to be in for a terrible shock!

My father had always been so fit, healthy and strong. It didn't seem feasible. Mum had always been the sick one, not Dad. Surely this was a nightmare, somehow not real!

I put the phone down in a daze. It wasn't fair. It just wasn't fair!

I always said I had faith. Did I believe Dad could be healed of cancer? It was beyond the realms of credibility that this was happening to us. I wanted Dad to live to see Naomi healed. Now it seemed he might not.

Just how Dad felt when he awoke I cannot imagine! His pain must have been devastating. He had expected to live well into his eighties. Now this nightmare hung over him.

It was a difficult time for my family and whether it caused behaviour problems for Naomi is debatable. She had been seeing a behavioural psychologist around this time, but he had left about the time Dad was taken ill. I missed his approach. On one occasion, Naomi mortified me by saying, in front of Dad, "Grandad has cancer. He wants to die."

She seemed to think the whole thing was a joke. I could have quite happily let the ground swallow me up. Once again, the old familiar feelings raised their ugly head. I felt a failure as a mother and a failure as a daughter! Why didn't Naomi behave herself? I could have said that Naomi did not know what she was saying because of her disabilities. Inwardly, though, I knew that would only have been a convenient excuse.

It was whilst we were paying a visit to Dad that the Lord showed us that His hand was truly on Naomi's life and that He sends his angels to protect us. We were on the farm, meandering around on the haystack there, when Naomi fell from quite a height. Fortunately for her, she landed on a reasonably soft surface and, apart from being rather dazed, was relatively unscathed. The fact that she was a child at the time, therefore falling in a more relaxed way than an adult, had undoubtedly helped. Yes, we had much to thank God for that day!

Paul and I had attended a healing session in London regarding Naomi, led by a man who is a well-known evangelist. Foolishly, before attending, I had listened to the media opinion of this dear brother. Any faith that I had in him had unfortunately been dented and didn't recover in time for the meeting. A lady we met at the meeting advised us to see another brother for counselling on generational curses, which we did. The brother we were hoping to see was unavailable. The healing session did not go the way I had expected. I did mention my family's involvement with Freemasonry, and what had occurred on Paul's side of the family, but to my knowledge nothing of any great depth was investigated and I left feeling somewhat confused and disappointed. Paul seemed willing to go along with what had happened and that was that. The one important message I did receive into my inner being was that my heart was wrong towards Naomi and I needed to repent. This I have endeavoured to do and I always pray for the right attitude towards her these days.

Dad had chemotherapy and radiotherapy and, for a while, seemed to do well. However, once treatment ceased, he succumbed to the cancer. I now spent most weekends at the farm whilst Paul and Naomi remained at home.

As my father's illness progressed, it was heart-breaking to see him suffer. Here was a man, who loved his food, reduced to a skeleton in size. He suffered severe nausea, was constantly being sick and often had stomach pain. When I saw his symptoms I almost wished I could take his illness on myself instead. It was horrible to see someone I loved, so weak and emaciated and feel so powerless to help.

I prayed and fasted, hoping for a miracle. Dad was a fighter and tried to have a positive attitude towards his illness. I shall always be grateful for Reg Ashby who visited Dad at his home and spoke to the Lord with Him.

Dad died in May 1995. He had lived well beyond the two to three months originally given. I am happy to say I believe he was right with the Lord at the end. Frances had kindly agreed to nurse Dad and the fact she lived at the farm was very handy. Jasmine (a family friend), was also there for Dad and both ladies were marvellous at nursing him. Jasmine had to travel quite some distance to help look after Dad, and I am sure that he was grateful. Married to an Englishman, Jasmine's background was French. Dad loved France and this undoubtedly was a link that brought Jasmine and himself that bit closer together. It was good to know that Dad had been at home, rather than in a strange environment, when he died.

Mum made it very clear that she did not want Naomi at the funeral. She was convinced that Naomi's behaviour would be inappropriate for the solemn occasion. Although I fully understood her reasoning, it still hurt. There was talk of all Frances' children being allowed to go, whilst Naomi remained barred. I dug my heels in and a compromise was reached: Frances' younger children didn't attend. I felt somewhat relieved.

Time marched on and I was rushed in to hospital with severe abdominal pain. It was suspected appendicitis and I remember it well because it was the day before the longest day of the year. I could have done without it so soon after Dad's death, but I wouldn't be surprised if the shock of Dad's death was what had brought it on.

Whilst I was in hospital, Naomi's former teacher at Lynhurst Place, Marion, looked after her. Paul started work very early in the morning, so it was not practical for Naomi to remain at home.

Naomi seemed to be quite settled considering the circumstances.

It was not till August that things truly returned to normal. We had a marvellous ten days or so, first in the Peak District, then in the Forest of Bowland. The sun shone down fiercely. It was almost too hot.

Certainly, Naomi was not one to hold inhibitions. One day, she saw some other children in a stream. Before I could stop her she was stark naked! I would not have minded at four, five or even six, but at nine coming up ten it was not quite right. Yet other people didn't seem to mind. Perhaps, I was prudish. Then I worried that she could pick up a disease carried by rats. Yet it was obvious the stream was clean and surely, if there had been any danger, the other children would not have been allowed in the water. Yes, I am a real worrier. It was as if I could only be happy if I was worrying about something.

The new autumn term started and with it a brand new teacher. Naomi now had a young, tall, good-looking American lad teaching her. His attitude and approach couldn't have been more in contrast to and removed from his predecessor.

Stuart was altogether more humane, understanding and on our wavelength. Naomi even showed signs of interest in wanting to write something, which had completely eluded us until now. I was very excited.

However, just before half term, the problems came. Naomi became very cantankerous and refused to get into the taxi to come home from school. On the day after her tenth birthday, she nearly caused an accident. Naomi was sitting in the taxi at the back, when she managed to grab hold of the steering wheel and the driver's arm. This caused the vehicle to swerve, and the driver was left in a state of shock.

Needless to say, Naomi was now left without transport and I was in a total dilemma about what to do. A harness to hold her in was suggested. Once again, I made a stand, although I felt sure that Naomi would relish the attention and the novelty it entailed. We started to walk or cycle to school. For me this meant four ways -- going to school twice a day and back. At least it kept me fit and, when I was alone, it always presented the opportunity to pray. Fortunately for me, she settled down again and life reverted to normal.

During this time a friend and I attended a meeting at a local comprehensive school. We had been advised that they were sympathetic to children with special needs. This was indeed fully proven when Carol and I met the Head of Special Needs. It made such a pleasant surprise to feel that at last there was a professional on our side, someone who wasn't quick to condemn or stop you in your tracks almost at once.

This lady listened. She heard what we had to say. There was time for me. I did not feel unwanted or a nuisance or an intruder. I felt Naomi had a chance. It had been a long time coming, but at last we were getting through. Of course, there was one small problem...only it wasn't a small problem -- it was a major one. Where was the money to come from? What about Naomi's behaviour? I held my peace. Things would work out somehow, of that I was sure.

In November, we attended a special integration conference. At this conference they discussed not only integrating children at school, but also young adults in work. We heard about these young people being given proper jobs. It may have taken them longer to learn their trade, but in time many had adapted well and were an asset to the firm where they were based.

Of course, not all were able to cope with the responsibility of employment, but at least they had tried and that was surely better than so-called training centres, which seemed to serve no real purpose.

One woman with learning difficulties even owned her own house. She had a special arrangement through which she was able to receive help from able-bodied people to assist her in the running of her home. It was wonderful.

So much can be done if only society as a whole can develop a healthy attitude to these so-called 'different individuals'. It seems to me a tragedy that, from the Victorian era, we have lost many useful members of society to institutions due to sheer ignorance. May their loss not have been in vain!

The parents were there to support one another, but one thing we clearly had in common was uphill struggles and continuous obstacles to overcome. Some families obviously had suffered more aggravation than others and, inevitably, it seemed to be *where* they happened to live that either ruled or destroyed their dream. I can fully understand why some families succumb to the authorities, thoroughly disillusioned by the stress of it all.

It was while I was there that I met a woman by the name of Tess Armstrong. I had previously met her at a Christian event called 'Breakfast for Women.' She had moved her child out of her catchment area to another one. She listened to my tale and suggested that I endeavour to get Naomi into the same school that her child was attending. Naomi seemed bright and perhaps Oakley House would be more sympathetic to her plight, than Spitalfields had been.

I did not know what to think. Tess certainly had an idea, but was this what I really wanted? It was food for thought. We met up again for an informal chat. This time we had other parents with us. It was all quite friendly.

Lynhurst Place held their Christmas party as usual that year. As I have said previously, we all loved Naomi's teacher Stuart and this year's party was especially wonderful because of all that Stuart brought to the occasion. He donned a Father Christmas outfit and entertained the children as only he could do. This happy event was to reoccur for the next few years, until he returned to America with his English wife.

Christmas came and went. I was now working one night a week at a care home that I will call Tamarisk. This home catered for people with dementia and I was called to work part of Christmas, which made me none too happy.

The new term began and Naomi continued to make good

progress. Her reading, especially, shone out. She was the best reader in her class. However, when it came to writing that was a different story.

She held the pen the right way, but there everything stopped. She expressed no desire or interest in the subject. There were rare times when she blossomed. It wasn't so much that she couldn't write. It was the fact that she did not want to. I would just have to learn to be patient. I started to get a new statement together for Naomi.

This was not as easy as I expected, but then things rarely are. Why did I want a new statement? What was the purpose of it? I felt like screaming! If it were the other way around, if she were getting worse, things would be different.

I was advised to get evidence from other people to back me up. I was looking for integration and they knew it. We all knew it. Of course, at completely the worst possible time for Naomi to throw a tantrum, bad behaviour once again resurfaced, especially around getting into the taxi! It was as if the devil knew what I was trying to achieve and he did not like it. Was it the fact that Naomi didn't want to change schools? Should I leave her in Lynhurst Place after all? Her happiness was paramount. I was in a dilemma. I wanted integration so much, but in spite of my dream, Naomi's interests still had to come first.

On the other hand, was it because Naomi wanted to attend normal school and was frustrated because this idea was not being entertained? Of course, it was quite possible that her recent spell of bad behaviour had nothing to do with either of these causes.

Indeed, in my search for the truth, I came to the conclusion that it was probably nothing to do with worries about school and more that Naomi had sensed a tension between Paul and me, which had manifested itself in an abrupt and painful way. Naomi had felt the atmosphere and it had left her feeling very insecure and unhappy.

I was beginning to recognise that I needed to exercise the art of self-control. I had a tendency to allow myself to be wound up. I shouted easily. I knew it was not going to be easy but, with the Lord's help, was confident I could master my weaknesses.

"How can I get my daughter to respect me?" I asked Him. "What is the answer to this difficult question?"

She needed to feel loved, safe and secure in her Heavenly Father's arms. Paul and I had to sort out our differences. We seemed to be working at cross-purposes. I was pulling the string one-way and Paul the other.

Tess, the woman I had met at the integration conference, had experienced this problem herself. In her opinion, our children are more sensitive, sensing tension more than so-called 'normal' youngsters. Indeed, I have since discovered there are generally more breakdowns of relationships where children with disabilities are involved.

Naomi saw the psychologist again. Her mental age seemed to vary depending on what she was being assessed for: her comprehension was on the four year old level, however, her reading was up to a six or seven year old level. Again, when it came to scoring on the computer, her age level was higher, at approximately a ten year-old range.

It was slow, but Naomi had progressed. No doubt about it. Other people had recognised this too. It had been a long, hard slog.

The year after dad died, we managed to integrate Naomi into a primary school. It was only a two-hour weekly session, but at least it was a start. Naomi was only there for a few months and they were far from easy. She was reviewed continually and there were plenty of ups and downs. Yet, this time, the news was positive. With everybody pulling together, it made the atmosphere so very different from previous occasions. Through this experience, Naomi successfully made a friend called Ruth and also bonded with Ruth's sister, Sarah. This, at last, meant that she had two normal friends instead of all disabled ones. Naomi was able to see Ruth here in our own home and sometimes at Ruth's home.

Naomi was transferred to a local secondary school for inclusion, at the appropriate age. It was not ideal, because the pupils she had known previously were now attending another school. She would have to make friends all over again. Unfortunately, after a few months, it was decided the inclusion was not working. We tried to fight it, but it seemed to be to no avail. The years of fighting had taken their toll. I could not face it anymore.

Now, as I look back, I wonder why on earth I failed to pursue my heartfelt dream. Why didn't I push for integration at Osborne House School? After all, they had so understood her problem there. Was it the fact that the education authorities had insisted Osborne House was not in our catchment area and therefore no funds were available? Was it because

I was now busy working? Maybe I did not want the extra pressure and the time-consuming hassle of making Osborne House become a reality! Yet possibly, and most likely, it was a subconscious fear of failure and of what seemed 'the inevitable.' I had become so accustomed to failure that to expect otherwise seemed totally unrealistic. However, I can only say I look back with regret. I wish now that, somehow, my thinking had been different. We all have to make choices in our lives and it is so important that, as Christians, we go to the Lord and seek Him with all our heart. The problems we face today may well be the result of wrong decisions we made yesterday. How vital it is to have a close relationship with the Lord! Christians pray, but are we really seeking God every day for guidance? It says in the Scripture, "*Draw close to God, and He will draw close to you*" (*James 4:8* (*New American Standard Bible*). We would do well to meditate on such a truth.

I like to think we learn from our mistakes. If we learn from our mistakes, they have not all been in vain.

Naomi's speech was developing well and her reading was steadily improving. In early June 1996, we decided to go to an agriculture show in our area and, for a while, visited it practically every year. As a young girl I had often been to another agriculture show in East Anglia, having come from a farming background. This particular year stands out, as it was an extremely hot day for the event and we were glad to look at some new Toyota cars and to get inside them -- the sales people were showing the benefit of having air-conditioning in one's car! It was also the year we opted to treat Naomi to some pets. We saw some rabbits and were told by their owners that, if we were interested, we could go to their farm near Bury St Edmunds with a view to obtaining these delightful rabbits' offspring.

A little while after this we collected the rabbits, which were both females, we were informed. Sometime later we discovered these rabbits were parents, with babies of their own! Although we hadn't planned for this, in some strange way we were secretly glad. We enjoyed the rabbits for a few years. Naomi liked to hold them, but seemed to treat them more like toys than living animals. I, of course, ended up being the person to clean out their hutches and supply their food and water. Unfortunately, we lost most of the rabbits due to a fox attack and our sole surviving rabbit died about a year after that. I like to think now that Naomi did learn from having animals, about the responsibility that goes along with them.

In April 1997 we faced a major upheaval in our lives. Paul was made redundant after working at his firm for twenty-one years. That meant I was to become the main breadwinner for the immediate present. I increased my workload at the care home from one night a week to three. I found this hard going, especially when pressure was placed on me to work extra nights. It meant less time with Naomi, but I felt confident that it was only for a little while.

Paul started a computer course, which lasted about three months. We did not go far afield for a holiday that year, but had a quiet break, youth hostelling in Norfolk. It had been such a special time, until the morning we left - 31st August 1997. Yes, that day will stay with most of us as, of course, it was the day that Princess Diana was killed in a road accident in Paris.

I returned to work. Paul's computer course finished, but he seemed unable to find the confidence to look for the right job. Instead, he spent more time with Naomi and became her carer. He was often seen taking her out in the car to different venues, whilst I was the one endeavouring to improve her academic achievements. It seemed impossible to get the right kind of balance. Often I would be covered with guilt, as I was finding it hard to give her the quality time she badly needed. I began to feel constantly tired. The strain of working, running a home and looking after a child such as Naomi, was almost too much.

In December 1997 we all went to Lapland to see Father Christmas. Naomi loved the experience of flying. When we arrived in Lapland, we went to a hotel where we met Father Christmas and had a lovely meal. After that we ventured out on a sleigh, which was pulled by a reindeer. Naomi fell off the sleigh, but was unhurt. We also had the privilege of travelling on a skimobile. She loved the speed and enjoyed going through the enormous wilderness, despite the severe cold weather. Our entire trip to Lapland was a huge success, only slightly marred by the fact that Naomi started her period whilst we were away. It was just one of those things, I suppose!

My mother, whose health had not been good for years, was causing the family considerable concern. She seemed to have tightness across her chest and difficulty in breathing. We thought this was caused by a deteriorating heart condition and, in view of her age, that nothing more could be done for her. It was unfortunate, but Mother spent Christmas in hospital that year. This gave me an uncomfortable feeling. I just knew that it would be her last Christmas alive on the earth! Unfortunately, due to various circumstances, both my brother and I were unable to visit her that Christmas. I still have regrets about this. However, the next two months seemed to prove my fears as groundless. Mother appeared to improve and I had real hopes she would be fine. I even had the pleasure of going to the farm at weekends to visit her on my own. I enjoyed the sheer joy of getting away from it all. Those times are indeed treasured memories.

However my optimism was premature. In February 1998, it became obvious Mother was not getting any better and hospitalisation was advised. It was a shock when we found out the reason for her illness. We were all expecting to be told that the arteries leading to her heart were well and truly furred-up. Imagine our horror when the unwelcome news came back -- Mother had a tumour in her chest and had months to live. Once again, cancer had come to haunt our family. Just as I had felt with Dad, the unfairness of it all caused me anguish! Mother had a history of heart trouble. No one had expected her to succumb to some other illness. Just how much Naomi understood about the nature of her grandmother's illness is a mystery.

I changed jobs briefly, but soon became unsettled in my new work and returned once more to Tamarisk, the dementia care home.

I spent most of my free time at my brother's. Frances was kindly nursing my mother. Just how she managed, with four children to look after, I do not know. Mother was old and tired and died in August 1998. Jasmine had once again been there for my mother, as she had been for my father. You may wonder why I could not nurse my mother. I lived some distance away and, as I have mentioned previously, was unable to drive. Mother was at peace living on the farm and it would have been wrong of me to expect her to come to mine solely for my convenience.

Around this time, a woman called Rosalind was nearing the end of her life as well. She had suffered an unexpected relapse of breast cancer and had developed secondary cancers that had spread to her lungs and brain. Rosalind also lived at the farm and had taken on the responsibility of bringing up her granddaughter when her daughter had disappeared. I loved Rosalind and had found the walks we used to take together beneficial and uplifting. It was at this time I had the privilege of helping to win Rosalind for the Lord. I was just part of the jigsaw, as there were also other people involved. I am so indebted to the Lord for his goodness and mercy. Rosalind was baptised in a lovely ceremony, just one day before she died. We went to her funeral, which was a celebration of her life. The minister presented the gospel and this surely was a challenge to unbelievers. It was one of the best funerals I have attended. Rosalind's illness and subsequent death was kept hidden from my Mother, but I am sure they have had a lovely reunion up in heaven.

1999 and the year 2000 were fairly uneventful for us. Naomi continued to make slow strides of progress. She was fast becoming a young adult and no longer a child. We spent two holidays in Orlando, Florida, that she enjoyed very much. We loved the enormous buffets and the hospitality of the American people. Their friendliness shone through. Naomi appeared to love the fast rides in the Walt Disney complex, but I was somewhat more wary.

The first year, we went to Kennedy Space Center at Cape Canaveral. It was weird to touch rock that had previously been on the moon. Both years we visited Gatorland to see the alligators. On the second occasion Naomi got to sit on a baby alligator, which obviously had to have its mouth sealed for protection. We also visited the marshlands, where we travelled on some special airboat rides along the riverbanks. The excitement was palpable as we sped along on what seemed like thin air. We visited Busch Gardens too, which is well known for being both a theme park and a zoo. The money from my parents made this possible. The Lord's timing was thus perfect for this trip -- the September of the following year, the month we had previously travelled, and was of course the time of the Twin Towers disaster of September 2001. We visited the well-known American evangelist, Benny Hinn's, church but he was away. The security surrounding these churches was an eye opener. Police with guns were patrolling. It certainly makes our churches in the UK look tame, for which we should be thankful.

It was around the year 2000 that we found out about Kirdale. We heard through the grapevine that, once a month on a Saturday, a disco was being run for people with special needs. It was held at the local church hall in the town. Graham, who was in his early thirties, was in charge of the event. People came with their parents and carers. Graham had a raffle and prizes such as crayons, paints, bubbles and chocolates could be won. Graham had a heart for the young people and often joined in the dancing. Twice a year, at Christmas and Easter, a buffet was given with an assortment of sandwiches and other foods such as flans, sausage rolls and cakes. We also visited different local cafés at other times, as we often arrived early at the church where the disco was held, to join church members having their weekly 'get together' on a Saturday morning. Naomi was especially fond of Graham and was sad when he moved away to another part of the country in 2009. However Naomi continued to enjoy a friendly relationship with Neville, the DJ who played the music. Other people have taken Graham's place, but sadly we no longer go to this particular disco. Graham did return, to be part of the disco, although he no longer runs it.

I remained working as a care assistant for some time. It is fair to say that I felt rather unsettled in my job in those days. One thing I was relieved about was that I was no longer working nights. Although I was working days, my shifts varied considerably. One week I could be called to work only eighteen hours and another, up to fifty hours if there was a staff shortage. We were also expected to do an NVQ in care work that would involve plenty of homework. I felt frustrated. It was as if the time I treasured for myself was being taken away from me and I wanted it back. I also felt I had failed to take heed of the Lord's warning in the first place. It was as if, in the spirit, I knew the Lord was advising me not to do this course and that I didn't have to do it. I chose to make the decision that pleased my employer. Friends, who are we serving -- God or man? I am sure if I had only listened to the Lord in the first instance, I would have sensed his peace instead of the turmoil inside me. After a while, I admitted defeat somewhat reluctantly, and chose to conclude the course.

Meanwhile, Naomi was turning fifteen. Similar to most teenagers, she disliked going to bed at night and getting up in the morning. She started to love wearing jewellery and developed an interest in wearing makeup, which she still likes to do to this day. I briefly attended parent classes regarding disciplining her. I found this to be quite helpful, although its main focus was on much younger children. The years at Lynhurst Place would soon be over. It would be the start of yet another, as yet undiscovered, era in her life. "What would this new and exciting period bring?" I wondered.

Chapter Fifteen

College days

Naomi's last few years at Lynhurst Place were quiet. She was taught by a pleasant woman called Cheryl and later, by a gentleman named Derek. Much was taught about becoming more familiar with public transport, learning more about money and developing cookery skills. Naomi had a natural love for cooking and thrived on this.

The school regularly had services at the local Anglican Church and Paul and I were always delighted to attend, whatever the occasion or time of year. It was also a chance to see how much progress your child had made over the term. Every term, one child would achieve an award for making the most progress.

Paul and I were now attending another church, where Naomi was allowed to attend Sunday school for a while (although, when she was about fourteen we were told she was too old to continue and that some of the young children were frightened of her). Scared of Naomi? What on earth for? Once again, the knowledge that she was noticeably different was hard to bear. Still, to their credit, this church always involved Naomi in their children's activities. Another child at this church, who I shall call Mark, also attended Naomi's school. He suffered from autism and, like us; his Christian parents had been devastated, wondering why God could allow such a thing. Mark had little or no speech, so his needs were rather different than Naomi's.

It was around this time that Paul and I became aware of the Oakfields summer camp. People of all ages were invited to participate in activities, directly aimed at persons suffering from learning disabilities. It was mainly 'sports related', such as swimming, climbing walls, crab fishing, netball, walking etc. It also involved indoor activities like crayoning, painting, craftwork and a disco. Besides this, there were also trips of interest on the mini-bus, such as going to the local zoo and even going on the London Eye the first year it opened. Oakfields Camp met once a year in August. This meant Paul and I had a respite break from Naomi for five days. It was the time to squeeze in all those things that normally were impossible to achieve due to Naomi's demands. One year we managed to paint the lounge, other times I would spring clean Naomi's room. It was hardly relaxing! I would say to myself "Come back Naomi, all is forgiven!" The relaxation I longed for never materialised and I was relieved to have Naomi home for a well-earned rest!

The people who ran the Oakfields Camp also hold a function every Monday evening, which Naomi attended until she was twenty-five. This club (the 'Monday Club' as it is called) encourages young people with learning difficulties to socialise and involves a disco, which Naomi was especially attracted to. The lady who was originally in charge of this club also arranged a trip up to London at Christmas to visit a theatre, where actors with learning difficulties performed a play. I believe the theatre was called 'The Chicken Shed'.

One Monday evening Paul and I had the good fortune to meet Trudy and John Elford. They have a Down's syndrome son called Robert and are a Christian couple that truly love the Lord. The Lord had spoken to Trudy in advance, when she was pregnant, to tell her that her child had Down's syndrome. Trudy is a remarkable lady who has accepted Robert's disability with cheerfulness and a grateful heart. Life hasn't exactly been kind to her. She has had cancer, her father had Alzheimer's disease and Robert's health has often been a cause for concern. Trudy, through it all, has been a beacon, a source of strength and a light in this dark world. She has backed me when I have needed support writing letters, or in deciding which direction we should be travelling for Naomi. Trudy and John decided Robert would benefit from attending a residential college when he left Lynhurst Place. I also felt this might be right for Naomi, but Paul was not so sure at the time. Trudy and John even felt led to send us a substantial amount of money one Christmas, without any prompting from us. The gift was very much appreciated and showed us the goodness of our Lord.

The days were fast approaching when Naomi would finally leave Lynhurst Place. Naomi had been born in October and, as a result of the school year, was one of the oldest at the school.

Trudy had told us of the charity 'Kids in Need', which holds special events for young people between the ages of eleven and nineteen. We were invited to a party celebration in May 2005 in Brentwood. There, one of the actors of the TV series 'The Bill' was a special guest. The Kids in Need charity cater for people with physical and learning difficulties. They provide funding for what they consider to be disadvantaged children, to give them an opportunity to do something they have always wanted or dreamed about. Naomi loves animals, so in October it was arranged for us to visit Longleat and tour around with one of the zoo rangers, just after her birthday.

A few months prior to this event, in July 2005, Naomi had left Lynhurst Place. Incidentally, this was only two weeks after the 7/7 bombing in London. It seemed unreal: Naomi would be attending the local college! She would be doing a course known as 'Springboard.' It would be a two-year course and involve her being there four days a week. She would continue with her learning and do such subjects as literacy, numeracy, life skills, communication skills, help with crossing the road safely and transport issues. The ultimate goal was that, maybe at the end of the course, she would be able to do some kind of paid work. Angela and Pauline were her senior tutors. Angela, in particular, bonded well with Naomi and had a close relationship with her.

Around the summer of 2005 Naomi started visiting Thorpe Park, initially with a friend from the church. Bev, a talented musician and dancer, befriended Naomi. At that time Bev was part of a group known as Connection. The group specialised in singing and dancing, in particular. Her ministry was to present the gospel to young teenagers in a new and exciting way at schools throughout the East Anglia region. This was a very challenging and time-consuming task for Bev, but despite her busy schedule, she made time for Naomi and their relationship blossomed. Sometimes Bev brought another member of the group along with her. Over the years, other friends have gone along. We also looked forward to going to Pizza Hut at the theme park. We now miss Thorpe Park farm, which in the last few years has been closed to the public. I enjoyed the welcome break from the fast rides that they provided, but was sorry when that chapter ended. Everything today seems 'go, go, go' to me!

October that year came and brought us to Longleat. We were able to stay at Salisbury youth hostel and travel to Longleat the following day. We were surely blessed on that occasion with glorious sunshine. It seemed more like summer than autumn. Naomi enjoyed being treated like a VIP and it was good to be able to ask questions you would normally not have the chance to voice. We were also treated to a special cream tea. We returned home the next day, happy and contented.

Naomi continued to make slow strides of progress at college. She had never been close to any particular person in her old school, but now she developed a close relationship with a young man who I shall call David. David is a tall, good-looking individual with mild learning difficulties. He is into computers and likes drama and history. I think it was Naomi's good nature that attracted him to her. Unfortunately, the one day that I invited David to tea, Naomi started to behave in a very immature manner. She grabbed hold of me and forced me on to the floor, thereby gaining the unhealthy attention that went with it. Poor David felt embarrassed and awkward and their short relationship was finished. He had been Naomi's first boyfriend and it was such a shame that it had to end that way.

Naomi still enjoyed socialising and mixing with her peers. She started attending Gateway, a social club designed for people with learning difficulties, on a Thursday evening. Paul would drive us in the car and I would remain in the background whilst Naomi danced the evening away. Paul meantime would return home and have some 'quality time' on his own. I met Peter there, an older man of about sixty. He explained to me that he had been a resident of an institution until the 1980's. He had spent eighteen years there, which was quite a normal occurrence all those years ago. Yet it was obvious there was very little wrong with him. He was possibly illegitimate, with a mild learning disability, and had been adopted at some stage. However, on leaving the institution he had managed to hold down a job, with the help of support. He was now living in his own flat. Peter had even managed to be part of a band. He stood out to me as a real example of what could be done for so called 'handicapped' people, if only attitudes could change. Until recently, Peter was still in contact with one of his adopted brothers and continued to visit him on special occasions. Unfortunately, not long ago, Peter lost his brother to cancer, but managed to handle that situation well.

In the spring of 2006, I started having health problems and had tests for bowel cancer. Fortunately nothing was found, but I was still badly anaemic. I had time off work, but on returning, it was obvious I was suffering from stress and the only way to alleviate that was to make the decision to leave. I had no new job to go to, but just felt I could not take any more. As I had left work voluntarily, I was not entitled to benefits of any kind. Money was tight and finding a suitable job seemed to be an uphill struggle.

The social services were very helpful at this particular time. They listened when we mentioned the difficulties we were having with Naomi, and how I was suffering from stress. We had carers advising us how to discipline Naomi. Someone came at least once a week. Psychologically, it was reassuring to know there were others to turn to in times of need. Leaflets were given to us and at last we no longer felt alone. How much Naomi gained from such intervention it is hard to say, but for us it helped renew our strength and gave us the will not to give up. Naomi also started to have carers taking her out instead of us. Initially, this happened on a Saturday, but was soon adjusted to Tuesday and Thursday evenings (Gateway has now changed their days from Thursday to Friday). It meant a break from her for two whole evenings. It seemed like 'heaven' to me not to have to go and sit around Gateway disco for two hours.

Paul had just celebrated a special birthday in March. He had always wanted to visit the Norwegian fjords and the volcanoes in Iceland too. We had some money left in savings and fancied a trip to these exotic sites. We, including Naomi, could travel from the port of Harwich and this was set in motion. It was good to stop thinking about 'job hunting' for a little while. As we left Harwich, a local band was playing 'We are sailing' which added to our sense of well being.

I think all three of us welcomed the change in our daily routine. It was a form of escapism and totally different to the so-called 'norm'. We were on a medium-sized cruise-liner where the main crewmembers were from the Philippines. The Filipino people are renowned for being friendly and hard working. We soon found, as time went by, that we, as a family, and also Naomi as a young person, had a special bond with the waiters in the restaurant. Naomi, by nature, is a warm, lively girl who loves people. There was also the cabin crew who came in daily to clean the cabin. I felt spoilt and pampered. The stewards seemed to have a unique gift of knowing how to make the room look its very best, under what must have been difficult circumstances, considering they had to do many more rooms besides our own. I admired them and wished I could take them home to clean my house too.

We certainly had more than enough to eat at the self-service restaurant, where we would gather for meals such as breakfast, lunch, afternoon tea etc.

The holiday was only marred by one significant incident that fortunately occurred when we were all out at sea and not on any excursion trips. The sea we were in is well known for being rough. Other passengers were obviously suffering from the effects of the rough seas. There were sick bags all around the ship. Paul was totally unaffected by the turbulent conditions and Naomi and I also hoped we would handle the sea without help, but this was not to be the case. It seemed to me that we were on a continuous roller coaster ride that we could not get off. Naomi's stomach rebelled and I felt queasy. It soon became obvious that she needed medical intervention, as the sickness refused to stop. Paul and I had to arrange for Naomi to see the ship's doctor and nurse. After confronting the problem, it was decided Naomi needed an anti-emetic injection. This was difficult to do, as Naomi is scared of needles and she did not seem to understand that we were trying to help her. Fortunately, after much trepidation and some reassurance, the injection was given and thankfully it worked.

On that holiday we visited places such as Bergen in Norway. The weather on this particular day was wet and miserable, something that is fairly commonplace for that city. We also visited the Norwegian composer Grieg's house nearby. His house is in an idyllic setting surrounded by high mountains and a lake.

We had the privilege of travelling on the renowned Flam scenic railway and, following that, commuting on the mainstream express train. On this occasion we dined at an up-scale restaurant where the food was magnificent and amazing to look at as well. The salmon I found especially appetising and there were choices of different salads, hot food, and delicious tempting sweets.

On the same cruise, we were able to see the Shetland Islands, which I had always wanted to visit. I knew Lerwick was the most northerly town in the UK and had been fascinated, as a young person, to hear of that town over the radio. It was good to see it in real life. In my opinion, the scenery there is rather like the Yorkshire Dales. It is wild, with rugged moorland, devoid of trees but romantically beautiful.

We also visited the Faroe Islands, equally impressive in their own right.

Iceland was included on the agenda too and we visited its capital Reykjavik. We were captivated by the splendour of Iceland's volcanoes and hot springs and were also fortunate enough to bathe in one of its lagoons, which all three of us relished. Paul, especially, succumbed to its delights.

We returned home to a very hot summer that year. Sadly, it was not long after we arrived home that tension and stress began to raise its ugly head. Naomi was aware something was not quite right and we began experiencing trouble with our neighbours. We live in a semi-detached house where any loud noise is quickly detected. Naomi's bedroom backs on to the neighbours and, when she chose to start thumping on the wall with her feet, a nightmare began.

Both Paul and I felt at a loss as to how to deal with the situation. The neighbours had one newborn baby and a toddler. I felt so guilty and responsible. We even informed the social worker as the friction between us intensified, but nothing helped. Just before Christmas that year, after yet another major argument, I broke down. I wanted to talk to my neighbours about the problem, to suggest some ways around it, but it was very clear, that was not about to happen. I had always felt my home was a place I could relax and escape. Now, for the first time ever, I felt a prisoner in my own home. The way I saw it, the solution to this problem was to ignore the thumping, so that Naomi would become bored and eventually stop this unwelcome behaviour. Some of our relatives suggested moving Naomi into our third bedroom, since it was away from the neighbour's side, but Paul used this room as an office and it was full of clutter. Trying to get this room ready for Naomi would have been very hard. In the meantime, I was finding the pressures of looking for work, alongside our current difficulties, almost unbearable. I managed to sign off sick with the help of my GP and another doctor in the surgery, but when the problems with our neighbours continued I felt I was losing the battle. Trudy was marvellous at this time and put me in contact with an advisor, who presented the case that I was unfit to work. This man was very good but, despite all his efforts, he lost the case and defeat was staring me in the face. It was now April 2007 and I was beginning to wonder if our differences with our neighbours would ever be resolved.

I, meanwhile, was doing a computer 'Clait' course at our local college. I knew very little about computers and how to work them so concluded if I wanted a different type of work, basic computer knowledge was essential. Evenings were often taken up with this activity and, when I eventually passed, I was simply on cloud nine! I had been attending one such class and was nearly home one evening when I met our neighbour, who I will call Judy. A few days previously I had given her a birthday card and, that evening, we began talking as if nothing had gone wrong between us. I felt elated and light in spirit, as if the Lord had lifted a huge weight off

240

my shoulders and I was finally free. It was the beginning of a better relationship, although there would still be testing times.

Naomi, meanwhile, had completed her two-year course known as 'Springboard' at the college. She had done well and made some progress, but was still not quite ready to start work. She was capable of filing different items, though, and this was encouraging. However, her future remained uncertain. It was decided for now that the sole option for Naomi was a one-day-a-week course that would last for a year. We made this decision somewhat reluctantly, but it was better than nothing.

Paul and I also tried to get Naomi into the other college in town. We had a meeting with an assistant to the person in charge. We understood that Naomi would have to pay for her courses and were quite prepared for this. We believed we had gone through the right channels, but for some reason the whole thing collapsed and Naomi was left with just that one day a week at the original college.

Naomi also started to attend Petros, a church fellowship group at a nearby Baptist Church held once a month for people with learning difficulties. Two women ran it: Sara, who was a carer, and Jan, who was a pianist. Sara would read from the Bible and then explain and discuss the stories with the group. There would be singing, either modern day choruses or hymns. Sometimes, there would be opportunities for people to pray. The group would also receive pictures of what they had just talked about and, if they so desired, they could also draw and colour in the pictures themselves. Refreshments would be available, which helped make people feel welcome. For a while, younger people from the church took on the role of running Petros, but after a short break, Sara returned to run it. Jan has since retired.

For the second year in a row we went on a cruise of a lifetime. Paul in particular was keen to see more of Norway and we travelled as far north as North Cape. We visited the well-known island of Spitsbergen and the most northerly Post-Office in the world, where we were warned to be wary of polar bears!

Shortly before we were due to visit one island, Naomi had been unwell with possible food poisoning. We had arranged a trek with the tour operators to this particular island, which involved us all climbing to a very steep vertical domain. It soon became obvious Naomi wasn't ready for such a challenge. She had been poorly throughout the previous night and, although we had been hoping sufficient time had elapsed to enable her to recover, this was not to be.

The reason for this may have been that Paul had decided that, even though Naomi was already twenty-one years old, it would still be a magical experience if we were to ask the restaurant staff to prepare a cake to celebrate that fact, making the trip even more special and memorable. They agreed to this, without charging us any extra. We even took the leftovers of the cake into the cabin, which may not have been such a good idea -- this was probably what had unsettled Naomi's stomach!

However, despite Naomi's obvious illness, we foolishly and selfishly persisted in our attempt to carry on with the climb. Naomi remained unwell and we were forced to abandon the idea. We had a guide with our group. He was carrying a revolver in case of a polar bear attack. At the guide's 'common sense' advice we reluctantly agreed to return to the cruise ship. Sadly, we were to see no polar bears on the whole trip, although some other passengers did glimpse these magnificent creatures from afar. I considered Paul and I to have been fit at the time, but whether we would have made it to the summit is somewhat uncertain.

There were other interesting aspects to this trip. We visited a pack of husky dogs and their puppies. Someone had informed us that this type of dog was not particularly friendly, but when we saw the huskies for ourselves we were thrilled. They were friendly, cheeky, adorable and altogether lovely. Indeed quite a few of us felt like taking the dogs home with us.

I was worried that the twenty-four-hour daylight issue was going to be a challenge. It seemed 'out of this world' to have the sun shine brightly in the sky past midnight, as if it was normal daylight hours. Yet the people of the north are quite used to this occurrence for six months of the year and also to the subsequent six months of continual darkness throughout the winter months. I worried how we would sleep with no proper darkness, but all three of us slept unaffected by the light surrounding us.

The holiday drew to a close and back we went once again to the 'nitty gritty' of everyday life. Even though differences between Judy and I had been sorted, there were still unhelpful remarks such as, "They're back. It was nice while they were away." I felt saddened, but thankfully for us, no further unwelcome remarks came our way.

The job situation continued to be a big issue and I felt trapped as I struggled to find a job of my choice. The familiar phrase in reply letters, 'I am sorry to say', became very annoying and seemingly inevitable. Of course, there were many other instances where I was to hear nothing for my efforts. In the summer of 2007 I was offered a job at the local college. It was hardly of my choosing as it involved the rather monotonous job of wiping down messy tables, but at least it was a job. I was finding the stress of looking for work, as well as outside pressures associated with this, very difficult to contend with. My new job did have some benefits -- I was now working at the same place where Naomi was a student, meaning that I was always nearby in case of an emergency.

Working at the college was a great eye opener to me. I was appalled by the bad language and by the mess that people often left for me. The tables were constantly left in a messy state, more like a rubbish tip than a sociable place where people met to eat and converse. Cans half full of drink were often tipped across the tables and disposable paper plates were deliberately shredded into little pieces that sometimes ended up on the floor. Chips would fall on the floor and no one picked them up. Spillages occurred and were often unreported. It was usual for me to discover these unwelcome incidents for myself. It wasn't just the male species either. Women were often worse, to my surprise and dismay. It was a wonder, and surely God's goodness, that accidents remained a rarity. I was so glad to experience God's peace at work and was quite prepared to overlook the faults of my clients.

Yet, despite the troublesome students, there were others who I found it easy to relate to. I made friends with two mature students who were on a counselling course. Theresa, in particular, has been like a rock to me and has encouraged me many times when I have found it difficult to carry on.

Problems with Naomi had not gone away. Well-meaning friends suggested that Paul and I should continue to look into alternative means of tuition for her. We were informed that we should have attempted to do this when Naomi was about fifteen, or possibly when she first left Lynhurst Place at the age of nineteen. It was probably too late now, but it was worth a shot. We decided that, with God, all things are possible even if it seemed foolish and unlikely to succeed. As I have previously stated, the county where I live is well known for not being the most generous with money, but we were determined to do what we felt was in Naomi's best interests. After looking at different brochures and listening to our particular friend, Trudy, we were drawn to one particular college called Linkage, which is situated in the Lincolnshire countryside. Initially we weren't too concerned about the funding, as our first responsibility was to find a suitable college. We looked around the college on a parents' day invitation. It was very welcoming and the students had a diverse degree of learning difficulties. We had a meal prepared and cooked by the students. Other students waited on us. We were impressed by all the activities the students did throughout the week and how their evenings seemed to be full of fun and social entertainment. We were made to feel at home. A little while afterwards, Naomi was invited back to spend a few days there.

This first visit was to be unsuccessful. Naomi seemed attached to her bed upstairs and did not appear to want to participate in the activities. Her behaviour had let her down, but we could always try again. It was disappointing, but not necessarily unexpected.

The second time things did go a lot better and Naomi was accepted into Linkage. However, our difficulties had only just begun. The funding issue had not gone away. As far as the authorities in our county were concerned, Naomi had been funded to attend her local college and there was no more money in the kitty. We had friends' support, letters were written and meetings attended, but it was to no avail. Paul probably found it harder to accept than I did. I think he felt somewhat guilty for not pressing for the residential college earlier. I, however, had been wondering if the Lord was trying to speak to me through a recurrent dream I kept having. The dream alternated between featuring either Naomi or myself. We were away from home, in a boarding school, and felt unsettled and homesick. As you know, I had a short experience of boarding school in my younger days and had not been happy. Was that what the dream was about? I don't know for sure, but I personally believe it was the Lord saying that what seemed right from our point of view wasn't necessarily what He knew to be best. The strange thing was, when I accepted that Naomi should not go away, the dreams stopped.

Sometime after this Naomi was accepted for a two-year

course called 'Learning for Living' at the college. This course was aimed at less able students, with a view to them gaining as much independence as possible without necessarily gaining work at the conclusion of the course. Naomi adapted well and once more introduced herself positively into the group. Gabriela, formerly from Spain (she speaks excellent English now), had initially been apprehensive about including Naomi in her group, but at the same time felt drawn to her. Her natural instinct was proven to be correct. Naomi started to flourish and maintain steady progress. In particular, her awareness of road safety blossomed. Her behaviour substantially improved, which in itself was a great encouragement. It was therefore a great honour when, after her first year, Naomi was presented with a cup to say she had been the student who had made the most academic progress of the year 2008-2009. Paul and I both felt extremely proud of her. I recalled how, many years earlier at Lynhurst Place, students had received such awards and I'd dearly wanted that for Naomi, but it had never happened. Now, for the first time, my distant dream had been realised and both Paul and I felt so grateful. Paul was so delighted that, when it was necessary to return the cup a year later, he ensured that Naomi was first photographed with it by a professional photographer.

Paul, Naomi and I flew to Gibraltar to visit Paul's brother Gerry and new wife Suzette in the Easter of 2009. They live just over the border in Spain. We enjoyed sightseeing there and travelling to Gibraltar to see the apes, which are notoriously 'friendly' when there is food around. We saw the caves, where people hid from the enemy during various wars. We also visited a zoo whilst we were there, and saw the place where Nelson triumphed at Trafalgar. It was good to sample Spanish food – for us, a hitherto undiscovered taste sensation.

As September 2010 approached we continued to seek God's direction for Naomi's life. The college offered Naomi a further year at the college, which was very similar to the one before. She attended three days a week, on a course designed to reinforce all that she had already learnt. The goal of this was potential employment.

Soon after this, Paul and I attended a meeting in our area concerning a Christian charity named 'Prospects.' They have homes in different parts of the country and were hoping to start a 'centre' in our area. So far, due to financial difficulties, they have been unable to make this a reality. Finding the right place and ideal site has also proven elusive. We would dearly welcome this for Naomi, but for the moment it remains a 'distant dream'. We do know, however, that the Lord can provide a way where there seems none. Hallelujah!

In the last few years I have benefited greatly from the support and friendship of the members of my prayer group. I have met a lovely Christian, named Cindy, a convenor of the prayer group. Cindy is very kind and patient and is reaching out in faith. She expects great things from life and I am sure the Lord will richly reward her as she continues to serve Him. Cindy has been very encouraging to me during the writing of this book, keeping me from giving up, and her daughter, Helen, is helping me with its publishing. My heartfelt gratitude goes to them both. Ann, also in our group, remains strong and focused on the Lord, despite being in poor health. A few years ago, she had to cope with the added stress of seeing her sister's health deteriorate and sadly end in death. In spite of this, she has remained a beacon of light. Looking to the Lord, we know He can step in and do the impossible at any time. How 'we praying ladies' would dearly welcome the Lord's intervention at this time! Ann has suffered much and Megan, another member, has had many trials and tests as well. The Lord continues to give her courage and determination to carry on, to finally, I trust, gain victory. Val, another member, moulds well into our circle. There are other people who used to join us but, due to various circumstances, no longer attend. Sadly our group rarely meets today, but we are always there for one another in time of need.

Paul had formed a very close relationship with his pastor, Tony, who is originally from South Africa. Sadly, Tony has had to return to South Africa and we are unsure if he will be settling permanently in the UK again. Tony has been a great inspiration and support to Paul, we miss him.

2010 was a difficult year for Paul. He lost a dear Christian brother in Germany, named Ullrich. This wonderful man and his wife regularly sent us Christmas gifts through the post and kept in contact with Paul over the phone. In addition, just before Christmas, Mutti died. She had celebrated her ninetieth birthday two weeks earlier and had been comparatively well, until just before she died. It was good to know she was a believer and loved being involved in the church.

My job at the college changed, as there were now new contractors. The Lord knows my heart's desire is to be where

He wants me to be. Yet, sometimes, just waiting for God's timing and leading can be hard! We can become so impatient and discouraged, and personally, it was hard for me not to be over-concerned about my age when it came to work. The Lord did eventually provide a way for me to leave my job at the college -- to become Naomi's full time carer. Yes the Lord is good and He does all things well.

Paul and I continue to entertain Naomi in various ways. She enjoys travelling on the buses, trains, and boats along the river. Unlike me, she is not a home lover and wants to be 'out and about' as much as possible.

Naomi has forged a friendship with someone in one of the butcher shops in town. By coincidence, this butcher's elder sister is married to my mother's nephew Tom, and he, my cousin, and my Dad had used to regularly attend football matches at West Ham back in the 1960's. The butcher's wife, Sandra, is very kind and likes to treat the children to sweets -- Naomi is included because of her disability.

Naomi used to go to a pub on Wednesday nights, that I will call The King's Head. They held a karaoke for people with learning difficulties and Naomi loved to participate, singing songs like 'Money, Money'; 'I am sailing'; 'Yellow submarine', etc. Music means a lot to her, and she loves singing. Naomi was also fond of the lady who ran the group and they had a good bond. She continued to go out to a karaoke event each week for a while, despite the fact its formula changed.

Naomi still attends a college in town. She has taken courses such as 'Everyday Living'; 'Keeping Safe'; 'Community Living'; 'English'; 'Maths' and a computer course. Naomi also enjoys dancing and drama on a Monday. Just before Christmas the group put on a show for the public to enjoy.

Naomi maintains her cooking skills and also does craft and art work at a local café in the town. She is always kept busy.

We are lucky, in that Naomi has always enjoyed good health, which is why it has been so distressing that she has faced difficult issues with her menstrual cycle. When she was still very young, her periods often resulted in sickness and stomach cramps. More recently, her periods have dragged on longer than expected and we have been forced to give her tablets to stop the heavy bleeding. Naomi has previously undergone treatment by a gynaecologist, which involved being put on hormone tablets. She is currently on the Pill. Naomi has too many 'male hormones' at the present time and we are looking for complete healing from the Lord for this condition. Unfortunately, due to Naomi's lack of understanding having blood tests can present difficult issues, as she is very fearful. There was a time we would have to warn the hospital in advance. Recently, however, Naomi has become brave and less fearful regarding blood tests, so it is no longer necessary to contact the hospital prior to them taking her blood. It seems to benefit Naomi if she, quite simply, continues to be treated like a child in situations such as blood tests. She has a spray that numbs the pain, so she hardly feels the needle going into her arm. When it is over, she is presented with a sticker and a reward of food for co-operating with the staff. This normally works and we pray over such events in advance.

I would just like to add to this, how good God is! He has surely kept Naomi from needing any dental treatment. All praise be given to His HOLY NAME!

Until a few years ago Paul had remained Naomi's principal carer. He has been marvellous with her and exercises much patience. Naomi can be very demanding and is obsessive about food and other people. Some of Naomi's obsessions seem irrational to Paul and me, but to Naomi they are very real. She finds it hard to cope if she loses anything and can react by becoming hysterical. At such times it can be almost impossible to calm her down and communicate with her properly. Just recently, she has become aware of the emergency services and even rang 999. This resulted in the police arriving at our house, despite my efforts to dissuade them not to do so. They had to come to make sure that nothing untoward or dangerous was happening at our house. They tried to explain that this sort of behaviour was unacceptable, but unfortunately Naomi relishes this sort of attention. It is at these times that I have to be very firm with her and deprive her of something she enjoys as a punishment. Similarly, I have to be very careful and diligent when we go for a walk, as she has a tendency to want to eat berries and fungi as a way of winding me up. Prayer at those times is vital. Still, on the positive side, Naomi can be very kind and usually wants to pay her way in life by being generous with her money and showing affection towards other people.

As this part of Naomi's life comes to its conclusion, I would like to finish by focusing the last brief chapter on her future.

Chapter Sixteen

The Future

Now that Naomi is nearly thirty years old, the difficulties ahead seem enormous! What should one do when confronted with a young adult such as Naomi? Should she go into a special unit for young people with learning difficulties? Or should she stay at home with us for as long as possible? These decisions have to be faced and it is imperative that God's will is carried out above all else!

I have tried from a young age to share with her God's love and all that Jesus did for us on the cross. She knows she is a sinner and that there is a wonderful place, called heaven, which the Lord has prepared for her. At times she has taunted Paul and me by saying, "I want to go to hell" but I believe she does this to wind us up and does not know what she is saying. As soon as she has calmed down and appears to be more sensible, she will readily confirm, "I want to go to heaven. Jesus loves me."

Every day when I wake up, if I remember, I pray I will nurse no resentment towards Naomi for her backwardness. I pray I will accept her as she is, deep down in my subconscious. I pray also to see Naomi as a blessing and a joy, that my attitude will be continually right.

That isn't to say I think it's wrong to want her healed. I do. God has shown me it won't happen by me *trying* to believe and 'work up' my faith. I lay down my unbelief by simply believing in *Isaiah 53:4*, "*Surely He took up my infirmities.*" As I see it, I admit my unbelief, my weakness, and ask Jesus to nail it to the cross. I then have a choice to make: to choose to believe for healing or not. The decision is mine.

Generally speaking, I believe it is God's will to heal, but so often we get in the way. Nevertheless, I look to the Lord to reveal his will for Naomi through His Word. If I am in the wrong, I will accept His rebuke, knowing that He in His wisdom knows best.

A few years ago, we received an encouraging prophecy over Naomi for her healing to become a reality. This of course is wonderful, but we still have to be very careful that such information is genuine and not some kind of 'airy-fairy' wishful thinking. Nevertheless, I feel it is very important for us Christians to branch out and find out all that the Lord has for each one of us.

In this age of uncertainty, I would urge everyone to examine his or her heart afresh. Who are we really living for, the Lord or for ourselves? We need to be on our guard continually. This is a world of greed and materialism. Who matters most? As believers, we won't be condemned (provided we are faithful), but nevertheless one day we shall have to give an account of our lives. Are we ready? When I stand before the Lord, my Maker, I don't want to be ashamed of how I reacted to our daughter Naomi. Let me stand before Him with boldness and confidence! May He indeed say, "Well done My good and faithful servant."

A little while ago, in my prayer time, I was seeking from God why He had allowed us to have these problems with Naomi. I felt He was replying, so my character could be tested. This is hard for us to understand, but the Lord does not make any mistakes. As I live from day to day, may I surely be able to know the following: "*And we know that in all things God works for the good of those who love him who have been called according to his purpose. For those God foreknew He also predestined to be conformed to the likeness of His Son, so that He might be the firstborn among many brothers*" (*Romans 8:29*). Yes, let's not forget verse 29! Maybe I need to suffer in order that, in time, I become more like my glorious Maker.

I would like also to say, take care of your spiritual heart. The Bible says, "*The heart is deceitful above all things and beyond cure. Who can understand it*" (*Jeremiah 17:9*). Nevertheless we need to listen to our hearts, for it is through listening and seeking God that we will go God's way and not our own.

Another topic I would like to mention is societies, and even many Christians' obsession that our offspring fit into a particular mould. Most people want their children to be intelligent and good looking. I don't think there is anything wrong in this, as long as this does not become the be all and end all. This world, and everything in it, is only temporary and what really matters is where we spend eternity. As it says in *Mark 8:36* "*What good is it for a man to gain the whole world, yet forfeit his soul?*"

What about Naomi? We can and must spend as much time with her as possible. She must continue to feel loved and accepted, regardless of her academic abilities. She needs to know that she is loved for who she is, not what she or another child may have been. She needs much support in order that she will reach her full potential and thereby become more able to live an independent life.

Before I conclude this chapter I would like to voice one of the most difficult things that I have to come to terms with. I find it hard to admit that my relationship with my daughter is not what I would have envisaged it to be, simply because of her disability. When I see my friends having a good rapport with their mother I am happy for them, but part of me aches inside. My relationship with my mother could have been better and it seems my relationship with Naomi is somewhat marred too.

There is, as well, the sadness in my life that haunts me daily. Will Paul and I ever see Naomi walk down the aisle in a beautiful bridal gown? Will we ever know the joy of grandchildren? Of course I cannot tell God what to do. Such utterances would be wrong, but I am still human and I am being deeply honest as to my real feelings. Yet even as I go through the darkest valley, I must trust God makes no mistakes.

And what about healing? That, above all, is up to God, as I've already said.

Yet my first desire must be that Naomi will know God and have an intimate relationship with Him. I believe God has a plan for everybody, including those with special needs, and it is up to us to discover what that plan is. Let Him be everything to her! Oh how important that is!

Yes, surely the day is coming when we will leave this earth, to go to be with our Lord in heaven forever. Then how trivial this will all seem! Naomi's disability will just be a fleeting memory, as she stands before her Maker, fully whole.

Then, as it states in Scripture: "*I consider that our present sufferings are not worth comparing with the glory that will be revealed in us*" (*Romans 8:18*). Yes, I could not have put it better myself.

Thanks to God there is hope and a glorious future! *Praise His lovely name! Hallelujah!*

I would like to finish this book by inviting all readers who do not personally have a relationship with the Lord Jesus Christ to consider saying the prayer that follows.

Conclusion

The Sinner's Prayer

Dear Lord Jesus,

Thank you for dying for me on the cross. I am truly grateful that you took my sins on Yourself, so long ago. I admit my need of You today. I have sinned and fall far short of the glory of God. Please forgive me for all my sins, today. I ask that my repentance from sin will be genuine and real. I choose, by faith, to turn away from all that I know to be sinful. I invite You to come into my heart and life and change me, I pray. Give me a heart after Your heart and please write my name in the Lamb's Book of Life. Thank You for saving me. Amen.

Lightning Source UK Ltd.
Milton Keynes UK
UKOW06f0952311215

265616UK00001B/4/P